STEAM KIDS

**50+ science / technology
engineering /art / math
hands-on projects for kids**

by:
**Anne Carey
Ana Dziengel
Amber Scardino
Chelsey Marashian
Dayna Abraham
Erica Clark
Jamie Hand
Karyn Tripp
Leslie Manlapig
Malia Hollowell**

P.R. Newton

First Edition | 2016

ISBN-13: 978-1537372044
ISBN-10: 1537372041
ISBN 978-0-692-78236-1

http://leftbraincraftbrain.com/STEAMKidsBook

Cover design by Anne Carey
Book design by Ana Dziengel and Anne Carey
Photography by all authors

Safety Note: Adult supervision required for all activities in this book. Appropriate and reasonable caution is required at all times. The authors of this book disclaim all liability for any damage, mishap or injury that may occur while engaging in activities featured in this book.

The cure for
boredom
is curiosity.
There is no cure
for curiosity.

- Dorothy Parker

We dedicate this book to our children
because they inspire us
to try, to learn, and to teach
something new every day of our lives.

Table of Contents

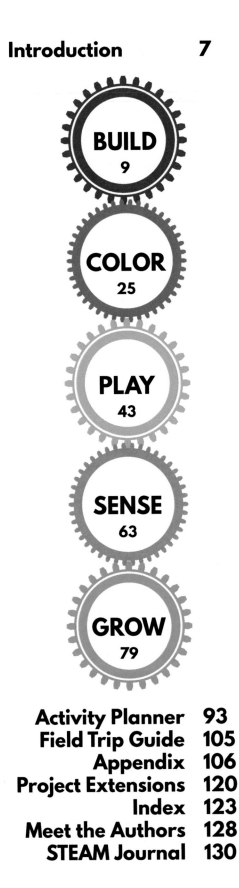

Introduction

STEAM - Science, Technology, Engineering, Art & Math

STEAM Kids is all about inspiring our next generation of
inventors, innovators and leaders to
question like a scientist | design like a technologist | build like an engineer
create like an artist | deduce like a mathematician
- and -
play like a kid.

We're a group of engineers, teachers, math nerds, art lovers and writers who all believe
that STEAM is important for children to experience and learn.
And that STEAM can be absolutely, totally, FUN!

Inside the book are 50+ hands-on ways to have fun with STEAM.
The activities are broken up into their area of inspiration: Build, Color, Play, Sense, and Grow.
Plus there's a bonus STEAM activity planner for classrooms, camps, school breaks and more.

We hope you dig in and have a blast
building rockets, growing crystals, eating polymers, and more!

What's the STEAM Behind It?

This wouldn't be a STEAM book without helping kids learn a little bit about the meaning and lessons
behind the projects. Look for the "What's the STEAM Behind It?" section to learn things like
the science of bubbles, the history of mandalas and the life cycle of plants.
Also look for the STEAM bubbles to see which category the project falls in.
They're perfect for when a child shows interest in a particular subject.

Difficulty

This book is intended for ages 4 to 10, but some activities can be adapted for younger and older children
with a few changes. The projects are rated for difficulty on a scale of 1 to 5 based on the average capabilities
of a 7 year old. Look for the dots on each activity, which will tell you what to expect. There's also an
appendix at the back with project extensions to add different challenges for children.

Safety Note

The projects in this book are intended to be performed under adult supervision. Appropriate and reasonable
caution is recommended when activities call for any items that could be of risk, including, but not limited to:
sharp tools, hot glue, chemicals, batteries, scissors and small items that could present a choking hazard. If
you are unsure of the safety or age appropriateness of an activity, please consult your child's doctor.

BUILD

Insect Hotel

Build an insect hotel for your backyard, then watch them come & go, maybe even nest

by Karyn Tripp **Teach Beside Me**

Materials:

Clay pot
Aluminum foil
Melted wax (candles and beeswax work)
Plastic drinking straws (smoothie straws work best)
Twine

Difficulty: ● ● ●

Estimated Project Time: 20 minutes

What's the STEAM behind it?

This project is a great nature activity since it focuses on observing insects without capturing them. Plus, the building aspect of it adds in some engineering and art can be incorporated by painting and decorating the hotel. It also takes some math skills to determine the number of straws needed and the height of the straws.

S T E A M

Instructions:

1. Decide how many straws it will take to full the inside of your pot. This will vary depending on the size of your straws and the size of your pot.

2. Measure the hight of your pot and cut the straws to be a little shorter than the pot when placed inside of it.

3. Tie the straws into small bundles to keep them together.

4. Melt a wax candle or some beeswax in a microwave or a double boiler.

5. Line the inside of the pot with foil and pour the wax into the bottom of the pot.

6. Place the straw bundles into the pot and press into the wax.

7. Let the wax cool completely.

8. Find a place in your backyard to place the insect hotel and observe it!

Project Extensions:

- This project works well for older kids, too. Add in an insect tracking sheet to have them observe which types of insects visit the hotel.

- For another fun bug project, try this Pitfall Insect Trap.

Building Challenge

Create hundreds of building ideas with this versatile engineering challenge.

by Dayna Abraham **Lemon Lime Adventures**

Difficulty: ● ●

Estimated Project Time: 30 minutes

What's the STEAM behind it?

Building challenges encourage children to discover basic physics principles and test their engineering thinking through design, problem solving, creativity and collaboration.

Materials:
Items for supports
Items for connections
See Appendix for a printable list of materials

Optional:
Drawing paper
Timer
Ruler
Pencil

Instructions:

1. Choose two items from the Materials List to use in your challenge. It is a good idea to choose a solid support such as toothpicks or pipe cleaners and pair it with a connector such as marshmallows or raisins.

2. Challenge your children to build a structure using only the items you have provided.

3. You can challenge them to do this in a particular time limit, with a limited number of items, or with a specific goal in mind (the tallest tower, the strongest bridge)

4. Measure, chart, or graph the size of the structures.

5. Finally, incorporate art by sketching, photographing or painting the structure when it is complete.

Project Extensions:

● Add complexity by introducing concepts like center of gravity and scale, or create design drawings before building.

● Create a Travel Engineering Kit or have fun Building with Straws.

S T E A M

Upcycled Toy Car Marker Bot

Put a new spin on old Hot Wheels with this fun marker bot

by Anne Carey **Left Brain Craft Brain**

Difficulty: ● ● ● ● ●

Estimated Project Time: 30 minutes

What's the STEAM behind it?

Working with motors teaches about electrical circuits and mechanical energy. The bots get their scooting motion by the vibrations of an unbalanced motor.

Instructions:

1. Attach a positive and negative wire to your hobby motor by feeding through the contact holes and taping with electrical tape. If your motor doesn't have a counterweight, hot glue a dime to the rotor at about half way between the center and the edge. You want it to be off balance.

2. Glue your motor to the top of your car. You can play around with the motor placement as the alignment controls the movement of the car.

3. Glue your marker to the car with the hot glue gun.

4. Next, attach your battery to the motor with electrical tape and tape it to the car.

5. Lay down your craft paper and let the cars loose!

Project Extensions:

● For an extra challenge, have kids create hypotheses for how the placement of the motor impacts the drawing pattern. Then test.

Materials:
Hot Wheels toy race car
Skinny washable marker
1.5V hobby motor (and a dime if it doesn't have a counterweight)
Electrical tape
AAA battery
Wire
Craft or art paper
Glue gun

Want more motor fun? Try one of these Brush Bots.

PVC Pipe Slingshot

Build a PVC pipe water balloon slingshot for summer fun

by Amber Scardino **Wee Warhols**

Materials:

Two 2' sections of
1/2" Schedule 40 PVC pipe
PVC fittings (no threads):
Two 1/2" T-shaped joints
Two 90-degree 1/2" elbow joints
Two 1/2" caps
PVC cement
Two 17" rubber bands
Four small zip ties
2 cup round Tupperware-type bowl
Drawer knob with screw
1 small and 1 large metal washer
Duct tape
Water balloons

Tools Needed: Tape measure, scissors, sharp blade, drill with small bit, handsaw

Difficulty: ● ● ● ● ●
Estimated Project Time: 1 hour
What's the STEAM behind it?

This is an engineering project evoking thought and design. It takes trial and error to discover the most effective slingshot design. Children can hone their math skills too with the "measure twice, cut once" rule in building!

14

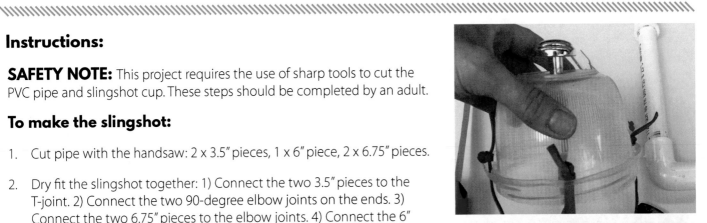

Instructions:

SAFETY NOTE: This project requires the use of sharp tools to cut the PVC pipe and slingshot cup. These steps should be completed by an adult.

To make the slingshot:

1. Cut pipe with the handsaw: 2 x 3.5" pieces, 1 x 6" piece, 2 x 6.75" pieces.

2. Dry fit the slingshot together: 1) Connect the two 3.5" pieces to the T-joint. 2) Connect the two 90-degree elbow joints on the ends. 3) Connect the two 6.75" pieces to the elbow joints. 4) Connect the 6" piece to the bottom T-joint. 5) Place the the two caps on the top ends of the slingshot .

3. Glue the slingshot together: Once you're sure of all the connections, reassemble with PVC cement. This dries fast; glue one joint at a time and tighten quickly.

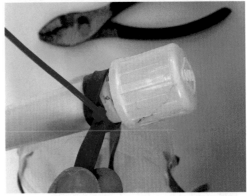

To make the water balloon cup:

4. Cut the two 17" rubber bands into four equal 8.5" pieces

5. Cut four evenly spaced slices around the edges of the Tupperware lip to fit the rubber bands into. Tie one rubber band on each hole.

6. Drill a hole through the center of the bowl. Assemble as follows from outside to inside: 1) drawer nob 2) washer 3) bowl 4) washer 5) bolt. Fasten tightly and cover the bolt and washer neatly with duct tape to make a smooth surface

7. For each rubber band attached to the cup, measure 6" from the lip of the cup and mark for a twist point. Twist each rubber band around the slingshot to the mark on the rubber band. Twist twice and add a zip tie, pulling it tight with pliers. Once it's tested, cut off the extra rubber band length.

8. Fill water balloons. Shoot!

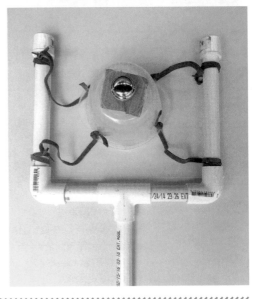

Project Extensions:

- To make this even more fun and challenging, you could try building a giant sling shot. Or try setting up targets for the kids to hit.

- Love working with PVC? Try one of these PVC Pipe Construction Projects.

S T E A M

Circuit Bugs

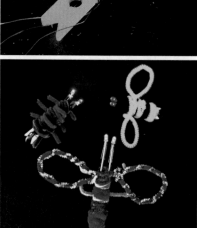

A challenging and fun circuit activity, with adorable results

by P.R. Newton **STEAM Powered Family**

Difficulty: ● ● ● ● ●

Estimated Project Time: 30 minutes

What's the STEAM behind it?

This project is a fun introduction to electric currents for kids.

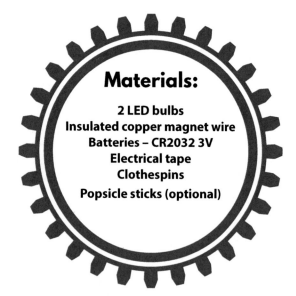

Materials:

2 LED bulbs
Insulated copper magnet wire
Batteries – CR2032 3V
Electrical tape
Clothespins
Popsicle sticks (optional)

Project Extensions:

● What other creatures or objects can you light up with clothespin circuits? Try trees, cars and more. Or try making a Squishy Circuit Jack-'o-Lantern.

Instructions:

WARNING: Coin cell batteries are dangerous when swallowed. ADULT SUPERVISION REQUIRED when experimenting with these batteries..

1. Cut your wire, leaving it long, at least double the length of your final bug size. Strip both ends of your wire, about 2-3 cm in length using scissors or wire strippers.

2. Wrap the wire around the positive pin of each LED, then take the loose ends and twist them together. Repeat the process with the negative pin on both LEDs.

3. Attach the LED to the clothespin by electrical taping one lead on each side of the pin.

4. Build your bug by wrapping the pipecleaners around the clothespin. Secure by bending and twisting the pipecleaners or with tape. Once done building the bug, trim excess wire.

5. Wrap the negative leads around one side of the clothespin end (the tight part that clamps shut), then wrap the other side with the positive leads. Make sure the stripped portion is on the inside. Then insert your battery to turn it on! If it doesn't work, remove your battery, turn it around and reinsert it. These bugs do not have an on/off switch, so simply remove the battery to turn them off.

Egg Drop

Design a contraption to protect a raw egg from a high fall

by Chelsey Marashian **Buggy and Buddy**

Difficulty: ● ● ●

Estimated Project Time:

What's the STEAM behind it?

This activity is a great hands-on way to explore science (gravity, inertia, and air resistance). It's also a great introduction to engineering, allowing children the freedom to design!

Instructions:

1. Use recycled materials to build a container to protect the raw egg. Decorate it too to add an art component to the project.

2. Place the raw egg inside your container.

3. Drop it from someplace high. Make sure to choose a safe place and have an adult present.

4. Check to see if the container protected your egg!

Materials:

Raw egg

Any recyclables- shoe box, newspaper, egg carton, cardboard tubes, straws, etc.

Tape, string, or glue

Art supplies (optional)

Project Extensions:

● Make it more challenging by adding in a few rules or restrictions, i.e. no boxes or parachutes. Or try building the lightest or smallest contraption possible.

● Like STEM challenges? Try this <u>Paper Plate Marble Maze</u>.

S T E A M

Paper Circuits

Light up an LED light by creating a simple electrical circuit on paper

by Erica Clark **What Do We Do All Day?**

Materials:

Peel and stick copper tape
3 volt coin battery, size: CR 2032
Small LED light
Small binder clip
Index cards, or other card stock
Pencil
Scissors
Art supplies as desired

Difficulty: ● ● ●

Estimated Project Time: 30 minutes

What's the STEAM behind it?

Creating paper circuits teaches kids about how electrical currents work. Constructing their own cards as an extension activity teaches the integration of aesthetics and engineering.

Instructions:

WARNING: Coin cell batteries are dangerous when swallowed. ADULT SUPERVISION REQUIRED when experimenting with coin cell batteries.

1. Grab a coin cell battery, 3V or less for safety. CR2032's work well.

2. Fold up a corner of the index card large enough to cover battery.

3. Decide where you are going to place your battery and draw a circle around it.

4. Starting in the middle of one circle place copper tape as shown, ending in the second circle. When you get to the corner, fold the tape over so that the non-adhesive side of the copper tape is touching itself. Alternatively, if you prefer to cut the tape, fold over the end pieces so that the metal sides overlap. You can hold the corner down with a small piece of copper tape. Leave a gap for the LED. Do not press the end of the tape to the paper where the LED will be inserted.

5. Gently bend the legs of the LED. Place each leg under the copper tape.

6. Place the battery on the circle, fold over the index card and secure with the binder clip. Your LED should turn on.

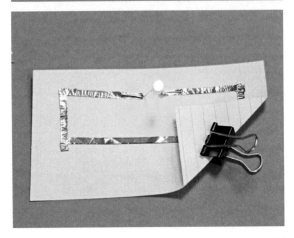

TROUBLESHOOTING: If the LED does not turn on, try flipping the battery. Make sure the tape is continuous and not damaged. Ensure binder clip is exerting enough pressure to maintain contact between the battery and the tape. Ensure copper tape has a secure connection with the LED legs.

Project Extensions:

- Design a scene that lights up and turn it into a card to give to someone. Ideas include animals, birthday cakes, cities, paper sculptures, or anywhere your imagination takes you. What happens when you try to create a circuit with more than one LED?

- Extension Project: <u>Aluminum Foil Circuits</u>

Craft Stick Catapult

This easy engineering project keeps kids entertained for hours launching marshmallows & more

by Malia Hollowell **Playdough to Plato**

Difficulty: ● ●

Estimated Project Time: 15 minutes

What's the STEAM behind it?

The catapult is a simple machine – a mechanical device used to change the direction or magnitude of a force. It is an example of a lever type simple machine in which a beam or arm pivots at a fixed point called the fulcrum.

Materials:

7 Craft sticks
4 Rubber bands
Hot glue gun
Bottle lid
Soft object to launch
(pom poms,
marshmallows, etc.)

Instructions:

1. Stack five craft sticks on top of each other and secure both ends with a rubber band. Place the stack on the table.

2. Stack the last two craft sticks on top of each other and secure one end with a rubber band.

3. Pull apart the unwrapped end to make a V and slide the bundle of five sticks as close to the hinged (banded) end as it will go.

4. Wrap a rubber band criss cross around both parts to secure them in place.

5. Squeeze a pea size amount of hot glue on the end of the top popsicle stick and press the bottle lid in place to make a launching pad.

6. Start catapulting your small, soft object into the air. 3, 2, 1, blast off!

Project Extensions:

● For a fun math extension, place several targets worth different point values around your catapult. Each time the projectile lands on a target, add the points to your total. How many points can you score in one session?

● Try these Stixplosions for more craft stick engineering.

S T E A M

Clay & Block Structures

Explore the concept behind brick building in this engineering activity

by Ana Dziengel **Babble Dabble Do**

Difficulty: ●

Estimated Project Time: 20 minutes

What's the STEAM behind it?

This simple project is a great lesson on how masonry structures work. Brick and other masonry structures are a combination of hard, durable materials, like bricks, held together with a glue called mortar. This project is a hands-on simulation of how brick buildings are made. It shows that they are strong and durable when built low and wide but how weak they become when built upward. Brick and mortar without some type reinforcement is structurally brittle.

Materials:

Air dry clay
(make sure it's moist)
Toy wooden blocks

Instructions:

1. Use small pieces of clay to stick wood blocks together.

2. Try and build as tall a building as possible sticking the blocks together with clay.

3. Experiment! How high can you build a tower? What happens when you press down on your structure? When is it strong? When is it weak?

Project Extensions:

Can you reinforce your clay and block structures? Reinforcement means adding in a third material that counteracts the brittleness of unit structures by holding them together. What materials can you use as reinforcement: wood skewers/dowels, wire, string? In construction, steel rebar is often used to reinforce masonry walls.

Need more unique building ideas? Try these 100 Invitations to Build.

S T E A M

Mud Brick Challenge

Challenge your engineering skills by building with DIY mini mud bricks

by Jamie Hand **Handmade Kids Art**

Materials:

2 cups of dirt
1/2 cup of water
Bowl
Spoon
Ice cube tray
Sunny day

Difficulty: ●

Estimated Project Time:
10 minutes + 2 days for drying

What's the STEAM behind it?

In ancient times mud bricks were used to construct homes as mud was easily available and an inexpensive building material. The ancient Egyptians used a mud recipe of sand, silt, and mud clay to create mud bricks. They also mixed straw with the mud to help strengthen the bricks they used for building.

Instructions:

1. Pour two cups of dirt into a bowl and mix in water a little at a time. Add enough water so the dirt is wet but not a liquid. If you add too much water add more dirt to it, so the dirt is wet and moldable.

2. Fill each section ice cube tray with mud. Pact down the mud firmly with a spoon or your fingers.

3. Set out the tray to dry in a sunny spot for at least 48 hours.

4. Once the bricks are dry, gently pull out of the ice cube tray and build!

Building Challenges:

How many bricks can you balance to create the tallest tower?

How tall can you build a pyramid?

Use your bricks and other found nature objects to build a miniature shelter.

Project Extensions:

- Create your own mud brick recipe. Experiment with different types of dirt to see which one creates the strongest brick. Try mixing the mud with sand. What else can you add to strengthen the mud bricks?

- Here's another Preschool Engineering project for young builders.

COLOR

Rainbow Reactions

Build a contraption that creates amazing rainbow reactions

by Dayna Abraham **Lemon Lime Adventures**

Materials:

Cardboard
Twist ties
Small plastic cups
Large plastic cups
Baking soda
Vinegar
Food coloring gels
Dish soap
OPTIONAL:
White paper or Canvas
Coffee stirrers

Difficulty: ● ● ● ●

Estimated Project Time: 30 min. to 2 hrs.

What's the STEAM behind it?

This project is a combination of both engineering and science. On one hand you have the basic reaction between the baking soda and vinegar. Baking soda and vinegar react with each other because of an acid-base reaction. Baking soda is a bicarbonate ($NaHCO3$) and vinegar is an acetic acid ($HCH3COO$). One of the products this reaction creates is carbon dioxide.

On the other hand, by creating a contraption that has to release the baking soda at the same time, you are introducing concepts of structure and function to your children.

Instructions:

Build the Contraption

1. Create a contraption that can pour 6 cups (1 for each color of the rainbow) at the same time. Cardboard and twist ties work well, but children can get creative with their construction. NOTE: Scissors require adult supervision for young children.

2. Test the contraption without any vinegar and baking soda to check for measurements and for alignment of the cups.

Launch the Reactions

3. Set up 6 large cups on a flat surface and fill with 1 drop of dish soap, generous amounts of food dye, and about 1/2 cup of vinegar. Stir together until well mixed.

4. Pour about 1 TB of baking soda into each small cup on the contraption.

5. Get ready, set, and pour! if you have timed and measured perfectly, you should get a beautiful rainbow reaction.

6. As an art extension: Use the bubbles and left over colored water for process art exploration. When the children are finished swirling and creating, use a blank paper or canvas, lie it flat on the bubbles and slowly lift it up. This will create a print of all the fabulous colors.

NOTE: This can be done in two sessions. On day one, build the contraption and on day two, launch the explosions.

Project Extensions:

This project can be easily varied by testing the combinations of ingredients. What happens when you add more soap? What happens if you swap the ingredients in the small and large cups? What happens if you use less vinegar? What other combinations can you use to make a chemical reaction?

For more rainbow science, try these Rainbow Reactions.

Number Art

Create art by exploring the relationships between numbers

by Leslie Manlapig **Pink Stripey Socks**

Difficulty: ● ●

Estimated Project Time: 10 minutes

What's the STEAM behind it?

Art & math combine when kids practice number recognition, pattern-making, and arithmetic while making colorful, modern artwork.

Materials:
Circle stickers
8 1/2" x 11" paper
Pen or pencil
Printable (optional, see Appendix)

Project Extensions:

● Try creating more complex designs by combining the different methods.

● Show how art and math combine with these Pi Day activities.

Instructions:

1. Create a 5x5 grid, making sure that the individual squares are big enough to fit your stickers. Write the #'s 1-25 in your grid. Or print out the number grid printable.

2. Use stickers to fill out your number chart! Here are some ways to do this:

• **Find the number:** Kids can cover numbers as you call them out.

• **Recreate a picture:** Design a picture with colors beforehand with each color assigned a number. Kids can "sticker by number" and when they are done, an image should appear!

• **Greater or less than:** Create your own designs using the > and < concept. For numbers > than x, use one color. For numbers < than x, use another color. When they're done, have someone else try to guess the rule that was followed!

• **Make a pattern or find multiple**s: Use stickers to create a pattern (ABABAB, ABCDABCD, etc)

Color Changing Play Dough

This play dough magically changes color with temperature

by Anne Carey **Left Brain Craft Brain**

Difficulty: ● ●

Estimated Project Time: 30 minutes

What's the STEAM behind it?

This play dough gets its color changing super powers from thermochromic pigment. Thermochromic materials change colors when there is a change in temperature. Mood rings and lipstick use them these pigments too.

Instructions:

1. Pick your color combo of pigment and food coloring. Two primary colors mixed together work well.

2. Combine dry ingredients in a large pot and stir until well mixed. Stir in water, oil, and food coloring until combined.

3. Cook over medium heat, stirring frequently, until thick.

4. Remove play dough from the pot and place on a plate or cookie sheet until cool enough to handle. Cover with a paper towel or dish cloth so it won't dry out. Once dough reaches room temperature, store in an airtight container or zipper bag.

Materials:
1/2 cup flour
1/4 cup salt
1 tsp. cream of tartar
**2 tsp. thermochromic pigment
(you can find it on Amazon)**
1 T. vegetable oil
1/2 cup water
food coloring

Project Extensions:

● Explore different ways to make the play dough change color. Ice packs, cold cans of soda, microwave, warm hands, hot coffee cups all make the dough change. Can you build a creation with different colors?

● Love the dough, try Color Changing Slime too!

Graffiti Art

Make some stunning graffitt art with the help of isopropyl alcohol

by Amber Scardino **Wee Warhols**

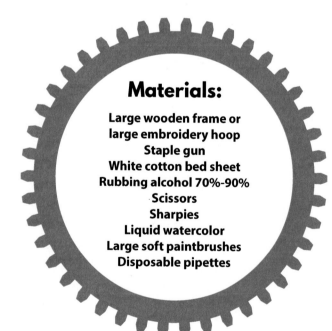

Materials:

Large wooden frame or
large embroidery hoop
Staple gun
White cotton bed sheet
Rubbing alcohol 70%-90%
Scissors
Sharpies
Liquid watercolor
Large soft paintbrushes
Disposable pipettes

Difficulty: ● ● ●

Estimated Project Time: 1 hour

What's the STEAM behind it?

Sharpies are permanent markers that can't be washed off with water. But they are soluble in alcohol. In this project, the alcohol carries the color across the canvas in beautiful patterns.

Instructions:

1. Stretch your white cotton sheet on the wooden frame and staple. Or if you're using embroidery hoops, stretch pieces of the sheet in the hoop and close. Cut off excess fabric.

2. Begin by drawing on the sheet with Sharpies.

3. Then paint the canvas with liquid watercolor. You can also use the pipettes to add the watercolors to the canvas.

4. Lay the canvas flat on the floor and then use the eyedroppers to apply the alcohol. This is a great way to work on fine motor skills!

5. Sit back and watch what happens! Talk about what is happening with the color and the science behind it.

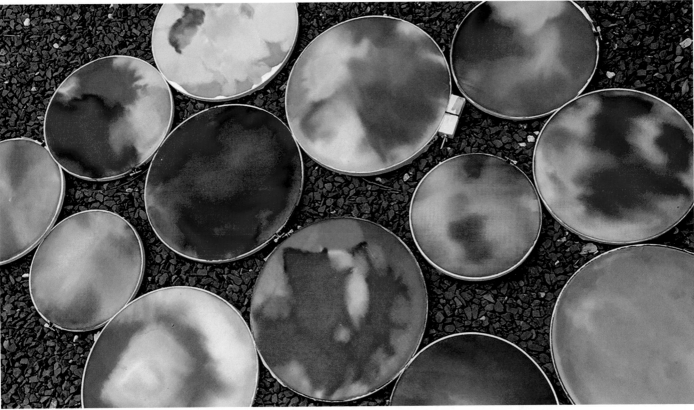

Project Extensions:

● Try making another project with the colorful fabric like pillows or try tie dying a t shirt with this method.

● Paper Marbling is another way to use color and motion for a creative result.

Oil & Watercolors

Try to mix oil and water with this colorful art and science project in one

by Malia Hollowell **Playdough to Plato**

Difficulty: ●

Estimated Project Time: 30 minutes

What's the STEAM behind it?

Oil and water don't mix. Why? There are more molecules in one drop of water than in one drop of oil. Since water is more dense than oil, it drops to the bottom and the oil floats on top.

Materials:

**Cookie sheet
Watercolor paper
Liquid watercolors or
food coloring
Bowls
Eye droppers or pipettes
Cooking oil
Paper towels**

Instructions:

1. Squeeze several drops of watercolor or food color into each bowl and dilute it with about 1/4 cup of water.

2. Add a pipette to each bowl to keep the colors separate.

3. Pour 1/4 cup of oil into another bowl and add a pipette.

4. Place the watercolor paper in the center of the cookie tray to contain the mess.

5. Starting with the oil, use the pipette to place a dozen or more drops around the paper.

6. Squeeze drops of color on top of the oil and watch it bead up on the surface.

7. Continue adding color until the picture is complete. Soak up any large puddles with a paper towel and let dry.

Project Extensions:

- Explore color mixing of the three primary colors to see what secondary colors you can create.
- Try experimenting with Oil Pastels & Watercolors for another artistic solubility project.

Glow Stick Light Painting

Make art by moving light so fast that it tricks the eye

by Jamie Hand **Handmade Kids Art**

Difficulty: ● ● ● ●

Estimated Project Time: 20 minutes

What's the STEAM behind it?

Shutter speed is the length of time that the image sensor records the image or scene you are trying to photograph. Slower shutter speed creates a blur effect of a moving object.

Materials:
Camera with a slow shutter speed (or a Smart Phone / shutter speed app)
Tripod or stable base
Glow Sticks

Project Extensions:

● Try writing your name or drawing images with the light.

● Print out your favorite photographs and create a collage with your photographs.

● Glow Stick Engineering is another fun light project.

Instructions:

1. In a dark room, place your camera on a tripod or table. Switch your camera to manual mode or shutter priority mode, so you can control how long the shutter is open. If you are using a smartphone, try an app to adjust the shutter speed manually.

2. With a partner, choose one person to work the camera (press and release the shutter button) and one person to wave the glow sticks in front of the camera (be the light painter).

3. Start with the shutter open for 5 seconds and take a picture of the other person moving the glow sticks around in front of the camera.

4. Try another photo with the shutter open for 10 seconds. How are the photographs different?

5. Experiment with different shutters speeds and different colored glow sticks. How does the image change when with shutter speed and glow stick color changes?

Milk Plastic Bracelets

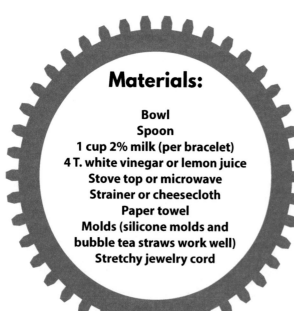

Create a special, unique bracelet using milk & science

P.R. Newton **STEAM Powered Family**

Materials:

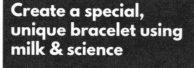

Bowl
Spoon
1 cup 2% milk (per bracelet)
4 T. white vinegar or lemon juice
Stove top or microwave
Strainer or cheesecloth
Paper towel
Molds (silicone molds and bubble tea straws work well)
Stretchy jewelry cord

Difficulty: ● ● ●

Estimated Project Time: Several hours + 2 days drying time

What's the STEAM behind it?

This is a chemistry experiment working with polymers. Polymers are molecules that have formed a regular chain structure. Milk contains molecules of a protein called Casein. During this reaction between warm milk and acid the casein molecules unfold and form long chains called a polymer. The polymer can be molded and shaped which makes it a plastic. This process has been used for over 100 years and is the way they made plastics before 1945 when synthetic plastics were introduced. Even royalty wore jewelry made from milk plastic many years ago.

Instructions:

1. Heat milk on the stove or in a microwave, just until steaming. Remove from the heat. Add 4 tsp of vinegar or lemon juice and stir gently. You will notice that it immediately begins to curdle. Stir gently for approximately one minute for the full reaction to finish and all the curds to form.

2. Strain off the whey (liquid) using a strainer or cheesecloth. Gently push the curds around in the strainer to ensure you've removed as much liquid as possible. Now remove the curds and place them on a few layers of paper towel. Carefully pat and squish to remove more liquid. You may need to replace the paper towel and repeat a few times to remove as much liquid as possible. You will notice it is kind of crumbly and squishy, but you can smoosh and shape it.

3. Now place the curds in a small bowl and add fresh vinegar. Let it soak for an hour. This second step results in a brighter white and smoother finished product. This is also the time to add some food coloring if you wish to color the whole batch one color instead of painting it later on.

4. After the hour is up, remove the curds from the vinegar and repeat the process of pressing them between paper towel sheets to remove as much liquid as possible. Knead and press the curds until no more liquid is being released.

5. Fill your molds. To make the beads use a bubble tea straw, pack the curds into the straw as tightly as possible. Shapes can also be created using silicone molds.

6. After 24 hours, gently remove the curds from the mold and place on a plate to continue drying. The cylinder created by the straw should be carefully cut to length (approximately 2 - 3 cm). At this point you can create the holes by carefully inserting a toothpick or drill bit through the center. Make the holes a little larger than you will need for your threading, as the milk plastic will shrink as it continues drying.

7. Let them set for another 24 hours (or longer), before painting and stringing on the elastic jewelry cording.

Project Extensions:

- What else can you make with milk plastic? Toys? Figures? Wearables? Give something a try. There are few more ideas in this Milk Plastic post.

Rotational Symmetry Art

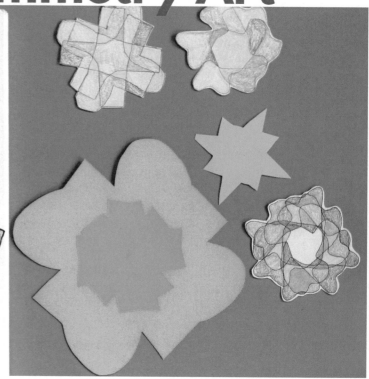

Create art by exploring the mathematical concept of rotational symmetry

by Erica Clark **What Do We Do All Day?**

Difficulty: ● ●

Estimated Project Time: 30 minutes

What's the STEAM behind it?

Rotational symmetry blends art, design and math. The mathematical concept of symmetry plays an important role in many traditional art forms from around the world.

Materials:

Paper
Pencil
Push pin
Cardboard
Scissors
Art supplies

Project Extensions:

● Kids can compare the rotational symmetry of irregular and regular shapes, and explore what happens when they include more, or fewer, than 4 rotations. Find more Math Art here.

Instructions:

1. Draw a shape on the cardboard. It can be regular or irregular. Cut out shape.

2. Place an extra piece of cardboard under your paper. Place cardboard shape on top of paper. Using the push pin, pin the cardboard shape to the paper. The cardboard under your paper will protect your work surface and help to secure the shape during the rotation.

3. Trace the shape. Turn your shape a quarter turn. Trace the shape again. Repeat quarter turn rotation until you have traced the shape four times in total. Remove push pin and cardboard.

4. Decorate as desired.

S T E A M

Prism Play

Explore light refraction with prisms and turn your discoveries into colorful art

by Chelsey Marashian **Buggy and Buddy**

Difficulty: ●

Estimated Project Time: 20 minutes

What's the STEAM behind it?

Prisms cause light to refract and each wavelength of light bends at a different angle, separating the light into a spectrum of color.

Instructions:

1. Set out the materials & invite your child to explore the triangular prism. How does it feel? What does it look like?

2. Look through your prism. What do you see?

3. Place the prism on patterned papers. What do you notice?

4. Hold the prism in sunlight. Can you make a rainbow? Place some blank white paper where you rainbow is located. Observe the colors you see on your white paper.

5. Use coloring materials to color over your light rainbow onto the white paper. Add other details to your rainbow drawing and display your colorful artwork!

Materials:

Triangular prisms (Optional: Other shaped prisms)
Small pieces of patterned paper (like scrapbooking paper)
Plain white paper

Project Extensions:

● Try to aim the prism's rainbow on a particular spot by building a paper or cardboard base.

● For more creative light science, try this Light Pattern Box.

S T E A M

Bleeding Blossoms

Learn about capillary action and the properties of materials in this science art project

by Ana Dziengel **Babble Dabble Do**

Difficulty: ● ● ●

Estimated Project Time: 1 day

What's the STEAM behind it?

This experiment illustrates two scientific concepts:

Properties of materials: When you spray the folded blossoms with water you are watching what happens when the fibers of wood (paper is made from wood pulp) come into contact with water: they swell and expand. The flower appears to open as the paper fibers swell when water touches them.

Capillary action: As the flower sits in the cup of water overnight, the paper towel surrounding the stem absorbs water through capillary action, the ability of liquid to flow against gravity through other materials. The water continues to "move" the ink on the blossoms outward, and by the end of this experiment the designs you drew will have disappeared and the ink will be gathered at the flower tips.

Materials:

**Template
(see Appendix)
Paper
Water soluble markers
6" Bamboo skewer
Spray bottle with water
Paper towel
Wood bead
Cup**

S T E A M

Instructions:

1. Print out the template.

2. Color the center portion of the blossoms with markers.

3. Cut out blossoms.

4. Thread three blossoms on a 6" bamboo skewer. Place a wood bead at the end to hold everything in place.

5. Wrap a paper towel around the skewer below the blossoms. Be sure it is touching the lowest blossom.

6. Close the flower by gently folding the blossoms along the dotted lines.

7. Place the paper towel covered stem in a cup with 1" of water at the bottom.

8. Spray the flower with a mist of water and watch the blossom open!

9. Leave the flower in the cup overnight and watch the color dissipate as water is absorbed first by the paper towel and then by the paper blossoms.

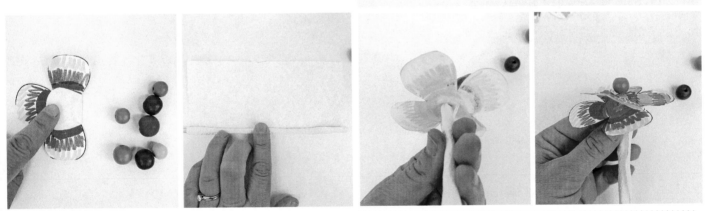

Project Extensions:

- Try using different types or paper and see how it effects the capillary action. You can try cardstock and coffee filters.

- Limit the marker colors to red, blue, and yellow and turn this into a color mixing experiment! As the red, blue, and yellow colors move along the blossoms, secondary colors should appear when the primary colors mix.

- Kirigami Water Blossoms are another cool way to watch absorption in action.

3-D Color Wheel

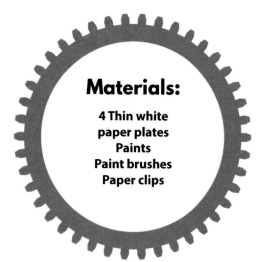

Turn paper plates into a bright 3-D color wheel

by Karyn Tripp **Teach Beside Me**

Materials:

4 Thin white
paper plates
Paints
Paint brushes
Paper clips

Difficulty: ● ● ● ● ●

Estimated Project Time: 30 minutes plus
drying time

What's the STEAM behind it?

This elaborate color wheel requires understanding
of 3-D engineering and spatial thinking. The colors
combine into a stunning art project.

S T E A M

Instructions:

1. Fold the plates in half and then into thirds. Unfold.

2. Use only primary colors (red, yellow, blue) of paint. The rest of the colors will be made by mixing the primary colors. Both sides of the plates will be painted, let one side dry before painting the other side. The front of each plate will be solid and the back two different colors.

3. Paint the plates in this way:

Plate Number 1
Front: Blue || Back: 1/2 Blue-Green 1/2 Blue-Violet

Plate Number 2
Front: Red-Violet || Back: 1/2 Violet 1/2 Red

Plate Number 3
Front: Orange || Back: 1/2 Red-Orange 1/2 Yellow -Orange

Plate Number 4
Front: Yellow-Green || Back: 1/2 Yellow 1/2 Green

4. Once the plates are painted and dry, refold along the original lines..

5. Fold the plates into a bowtie shape with the solid color folded inward. Attach in the center of the fold with a paper clip. Do the same with all four plates.

6. Match up the plates according to the color wheel with red next to red orange, next to orange and so on. Attach them all with paper clips.

7. Use a string with a large knot tied on the end and put it through the center to hang it up. Admire the color wheel and talk about ROYGBIV, the colors of the rainbow.

Project Extensions:

- Explore other ways to make a color wheel. Do a color hunt around the house or back yard and find objects in each of the colors. Organize into a color wheel.

- Walking Water is another way to create a color wheel, this time with the science of absorption.

PLAY

Bubble Trays

Explore building with bubbles. What shapes can you make?

by Chelsey Marashian **Buggy and Buddy**

Materials:

Bubble solution (see pg. 68 for a homemade bubble solution recipe)
Tray or cookie sheet
Straw

Difficulty: ● ●

Estimated Project Time: 15 minutes

What's the STEAM behind it?

In this activity children explore the science of how molecules in soap film behave when they share a bubble wall. Kids explore engineering as they observe and create various bubble structures, noticing how different areas of the structure can support and strengthen their bubble creations.

Instructions:

1. Fill your tray with bubble solution.

2. Place a straw into your tray of bubble solution and blow a bubble. How does your bubble look?

3. Blow some more bubbles near your first bubble. Describe their appearance.

4. Try blowing a bubble inside another bubble. What worked? What didn't work?

5. Try to blow a bubble tower. How high can it get? Where is the best place to blow to make your tower grow?

Project Extensions:

● Extend this project by creating your own bubble wands to use in your bubble tray. Build them using materials like pipe cleaners, straws, and crafting wire.

● You can also experiment with creating your own bubble solution using dish soap and water. What ratios work best? What could you add to your mixture to strengthen the bubbles?

● Try making Bubble Patterns for an artistic addition to this project.

Ribbon Rocket

Make a rocket out of leftover cardboard tubes and ribbon.

by Karyn Tripp **Teach Beside Me**

Difficulty: ●●

Estimated Project Time: 30 minutes

What's the STEAM behind it?

What makes these rockets move? This is a fun physics lesson. When the ribbons are pulled apart, the ribbons put force on the end of the cardboard tube, causing it to move forward.

Materials:

Cardboard tubes
Curling gift ribbon
Paint
Colored paper

Instructions:

1. Paint and decorate your cardboard tube. Let it dry.

2. Cut two small triangles out of colored paper and glue to the sides to look like the fin of the rocket ship.

3. Cut two long pieces of ribbon, the same length. They will need to be several feet long (4-5 feet). Place the ribbons through the tube.

4. Two people will hold the ribbons straight out, one ribbon in each hand. Push the rocket all the way to one person. They will quickly open the two ribbon pieces and it will send the rocket across the ribbon. Then the other person will do the same. It can continue back and forth across the ribbons.

Project Extensions:

● Set goals for the number of times they can race it across to each other in a specific amount of time. Help them understand why the movement is happening.

● Love rockets? Try these <u>Straw Rockets</u> too.

Roll & Cover Game

Work on math skills with this super sweet coloring game.

by Malia Hollowell **Playdough to Plato**

Difficulty: ●●

Estimated Project Time: 20 minutes

What's the STEAM behind it?

As children roll and color, they build critical counting, number recognition and addition skills.

Instructions:

1. Print the desired Ice Cream Roll and Color sheet. (One sheet practices recognizing the numbers 1-6, another page focuses on two dice addition and a third version challenges kids to add three numbers.)

2. Roll the dice. If you're working on the addition sheets, add the numbers together.

3. Color the matching number or sum on the sheet.

4. Continue until all ice creams have been filled.

Project Extensions:

● For extra challenge, children could design their own roll and color sheets! Or try using multiplication instead of addition.

● Add some science to the game with Ice Cream in a Bag.

Materials:

Template (see Appendix)
3 dice
Crayons

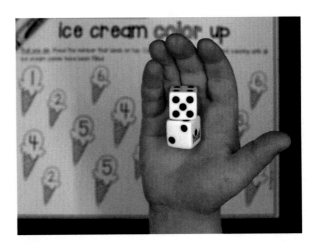

S T E A M

DIY Outdoor Tinker Wall

Design and build a giant ball run with building materials.

by Dayna Abraham **Lemon Lime Adventures**

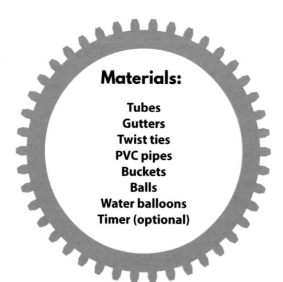

Materials:

Tubes
Gutters
Twist ties
PVC pipes
Buckets
Balls
Water balloons
Timer (optional)

Difficulty: ● ● ●

Estimated Project Time: 1 hour

What's the STEAM behind it?

Tinkering and creating projects are perfect for encouraging children to problem-solve and explore cause and effect. Depending on the age of the children, you can explore concepts of simple machines and physics with their creations. This is a great project to discuss the laws of science and math like gravity and angles.

Instructions:

1. Gather as many recycled building materials you can find.

2. Draw out ideas or just get started building your ball run.

3. Using a fence, a deck, or even the side of a play set, attach tubes and materials with twist ties.

4. If it is really warm outside, you can even attempt to use water and water balloons in your ramps and creations.

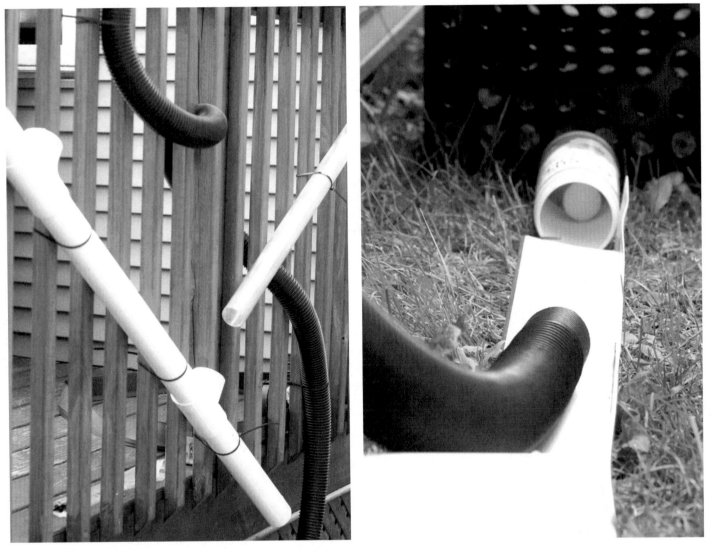

Project Extensions:

● There are no limits on this project. To challenge children, encourage them to continue designing new parts and machines.

● Looking for something on a smaller scale? Try a LEGO Marble Maze.

Pendulum Painting

Experience the force of motion with a new twist on painting

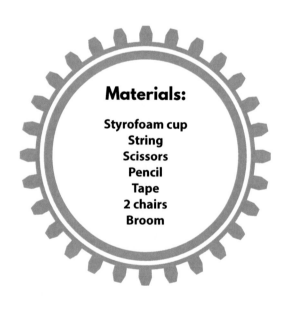

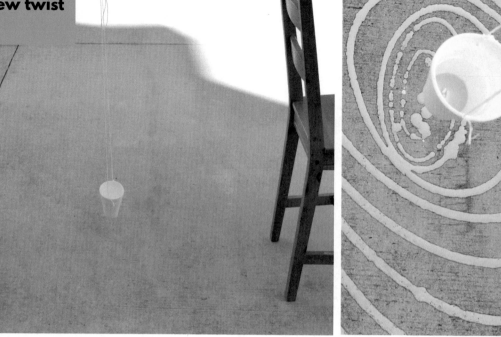

by Jamie Hand **Handmade Kids Art**

Difficulty: ●●●●
Estimated Project Time: 20 minutes

What's the STEAM behind it?

A pendulum is a fixed object hung from a point so it can swing freely back and forth due to the force of gravity. Another example of a pendulum is a swing.

Materials:

**Styrofoam cup
String
Scissors
Pencil
Tape
2 chairs
Broom**

Instructions:

1. Prep the pendulum by poking a hole in the bottom of the paper cup with a pencil. Poke two more holes on each side of the cup underneath the rim of the cup. Tie a piece of string through the two holes on the side of the cup creating a handle for the cup to hang.

2. Place a broom horizontally across the top of two chairs. Hang the cup string from the middle of the broom.

3. Cover the bottom hole of the cup with tape. Test your pendulum with water first to give your artist time to experiment with swinging the cup. Then empty the cup and fill with paint. Remove the tape and swing the cup. Observe what patterns the pendulum creates with the paint.

Project Extensions:

● Experiment with different lengths of string. How does it change the pattern of the paint? What happens if you swing the pendulum gently or swing it more forcefully?

● Gravity Painting is another fun way to learn physics while painting.

S T E A M

If-Then Coding Game

No computer needed for this intro to coding game

Anne Carey **Left Brain Craft Brain**

Difficulty: ●
Estimated Project Time: 15 minutes

What's the STEAM behind it?

If-Then statements are the building blocks of programming languages.

Materials:

Kids!

Project Extensions:

● Try using some of the great introduction to coding apps available for kids, like Scratch.

● Or check out these other Coding Games for Kids.

Instructions:

Pick one Programmer, line up the rest of the children as Computers and start playing this Monkey See, Money Do type game.

Difficulty Level 1 – If I Do This, Then You Do This

The Programmer commands the Computers to do the same thing she does and to stop when she stops.

Difficulty Level 2 – If I Do This, Then You Do That

Add the twist that the Computers should do something different than the Programmer, but still start and stop when they do. This one works the brain because they'll hear something different than they are seeing.

Difficulty Level 3 – If I Do This, Then You Do That, Else You Do Something Else

Next, add If-Then-Else statements. For example, the Programmer commands "If I raise my right arm, Then you raise your left arm, Else raise your right foot."

Difficulty Level 4 – If-Then-Else Speed Round with Eliminations

The Computers "break" & sit down when they don't follow commands correctly. The last onestanding wins.

51

Bedroom Planetarium

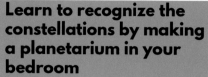

Learn to recognize the constellations by making a planetarium in your bedroom

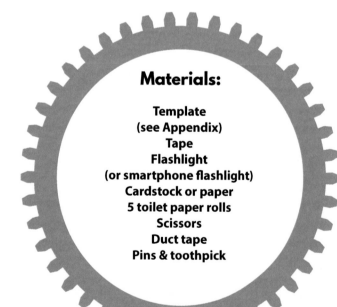

by Ana Dziengel **Babble Dabble Do**

Materials:

Template
(see Appendix)
Tape
Flashlight
(or smartphone flashlight)
Cardstock or paper
5 toilet paper rolls
Scissors
Duct tape
Pins & toothpick

Difficulty: ● ● ●

Estimated Project Time: 30 minutes

What's the STEAM behind it?

If you are interested in astronomy but don't know where to begin when you look up at a night sky full of stars, try learning to recognize some basic constellations first.

Instructions:

1. Print out the template on cardstock or heavy weight paper. Cut out constellation templates and cards.

2. Cut toilet paper rolls in half.

3. Cut a strip of duct tape and lay it on a table with the sticky side up. Place one circular constellation card on the duct tape face up.

4. Use a pushpin to carefully poke through the dots in the constellation. You can use different sized pins or a toothpick to make holes of different sizes to match the star brightness.

5. Place a TP roll over the constellation card and pull duct tape tightly over the tube end. Add duct tape to seal off light leaks.

6. Tape the constellation card onto on the side of the tube.

7. Repeat Steps 1-6 for additional constellations.

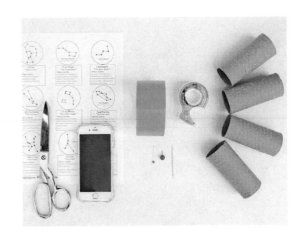

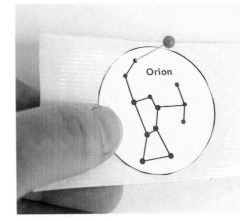

How to View:

Method 1
Hold the tubes up to a light or the sky and look into them.

Method 2
In a dark room position a flashlight to shine into the tube. Tip: A smartphone flashlight is ideal because it casts uniform light.
To eliminate light leaks, lay the Smartphone on the bed and place the constellation tube on top of it. You wil see the constellation projected on your ceiling! You can also project it onto a nearby wall.

NOTE:
Not all constellations are visible in all places at all times of the year. Some constellations are visible in both the northern and southern hemispheres, others only from one hemisphere. The time of year and the earth's rotation also effects what constellations are visible on any given night when looking at the sky.

Project Extensions:

- After learning to recognize some of the constellations, try going outside to see if you can find them in the night sky.

- Find a star map online and try making a planetarium for a larger section of the night sky to be able to see the constellations in context to one another.

- Another fun way to learn the constellations is to make a Constellation Geoboard or using a smart phone constellation app.

Bottle Rockets

Bottle rockets are a high flying engineering and science project

by P.R. Newton **STEAM Powered Family**

Materials:

Plastic bottles (2 liter soda bottles work best)
Vinegar
Baking soda
Paper towels
Cork
Launch pad made of blocks, sticks, LEGO, etc.
Craft supplies (optional)

Difficulty: ● ● ● ●
Estimated Project Time: 30 minutes

What's the STEAM behind it?

The chemical reaction between vinegar (an acid) and baking soda (a base) causes this rocket to fly. The reaction creates C02, causing the pressure in the bottle to increase until the cork gets popped out. Different cork materials give under different pressures, which changes the force of the launch, resulting in very different amounts of lift.

Instructions:

SAFETY NOTE: This project requires ADULT SUPERVISION and EYE PROTECTION.

1. Create a Launch Pad: Build a structure that can hold the bottle upside-down without it falling through. It must also be stable enough to support the energy of the blast off. Tinker Toys, LEGOs, craft sticks, branches, etc. can all work.

2. Prepare your bottle by washing and drying it well. If desired, decorate it.

3. Find a cork. With younger children you may wish to make your own cork using cut foam, like a pool noodle. This type of cork gives under less pressure and will fly 5-10 feet. With older children, or if younger children are watching from a distance, try wine corks. The pressure increase using wine corks is significant. Plan accordingly, as you will need a very big, open space. Wine corks easily reach heights between 60 and 100 feet.

4. For each rocket, place one tablespoon of baking soda on a paper towel. Then fold it up into a tight roll that can be inserted into the bottle easily. You can prepare a bunch of these ahead of time so you can quickly reload the bottles.

5. Set up the launch pad in open space, add 1 cup of vinegar to the bottle, slip your rolled up paper towel into the bottle, then add the cork. Quickly turn the bottle upside-down and place it on your launching pad.

6. Back up quickly!

7. Depending on a number of factors it can take time for the bottle to launch. It can be up to a minute, which can seem extremely long! Do not get close to the bottle as it could launch at any time without warning. If a bottle needs to be approached, ensure an adult is doing it and they are taking appropriate precautions.

Project Extensions:

- Replace the homemade cork with a wine cork for extra force and lift. You can also make the launching pad design a more complicated engineering challenge, perhaps using lumber, screws, and other tools.

- Explore more baking soda and vinegar reactions with these Hatching Dino Eggs.

Stop Motion Video

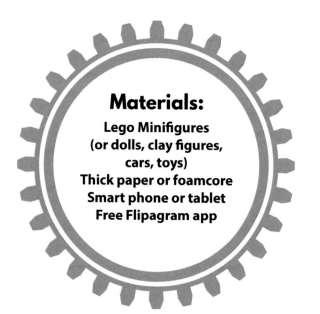

An introduction to the art of filmmaking with stop action video

Difficulty: ● ● ● ●
Estimated Project Time: 45 minutes

What's the STEAM behind it?

Stop motion animation is a fun way for kids to learn to use technology. Plus stop action teaches critical thinking as they have to plan ahead. Plus they are introduced to the art of film!

Materials:
**Lego Minifigures
(or dolls, clay figures,
cars, toys)
Thick paper or foamcore
Smart phone or tablet
Free Flipagram app**

by Amber Scardino **Wee Warhols**

Instructions:

1. Download Flipagram onto your smart phone or tablet.

2. Choose your characters and discuss a story plan.

3. Set up your scene/background using scrapbooking paper (there are cool ones available with beach scenes, city scenes, nature). Or you can use white foam core, which is great for contrast in photos.

4. Take a photo each time you move your characters. More photos and smaller movements result in a better video.

5. Open your Flipagram app. Add your photos in the order that you want them to appear.

6. Hit Next when you're finished adding photos, and Flipagram will compile your animation. You can adjust the speed and even add music!

Project Extensions:

● Explore other types of filmmaking as an extension to stop action filmmaking.

Candy Maze

Design and build a sweet maze out of gummy candy

by Leslie Manlapig **Pink Stripey Socks**

Difficulty: ●●

Estimated Project Time: 10 minutes

What's the STEAM behind it?

Designing and building a maze requires an understanding of gravity's impact on the moving candy and helps kids learn from trial and error.

Materials:
Gummy candies
Round hard candy
Styrofoam tray
Tooth picks
Scissors

Instructions:

1. Lay your candy out to create a maze design. Make sure your hard round candy easily rolls through your design.

2. Once you're satisfied with candy placement, use toothpicks to secure everything in place. Flip over tray. Trim off all the excess toothpick parts.

3. Place your round candies on the board and play!

Project Extensions:

● Make the maze more challenging by adding holes to the tray.

● Want to build another toy? Try building a Conveyor Belt.

S T E A M

Hare and Hounds Game

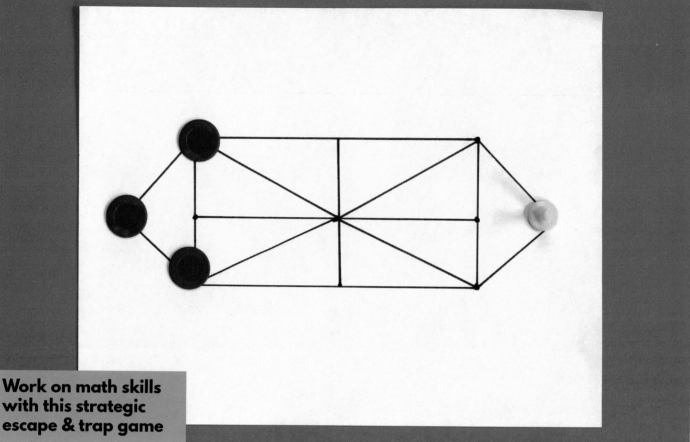

Work on math skills with this strategic escape & trap game

by Erica Clark **What Do We Do All Day?**

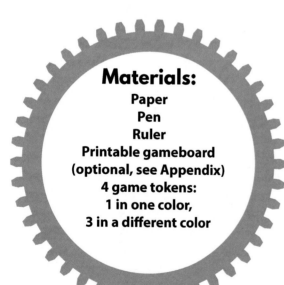

Materials:
Paper
Pen
Ruler
**Printable gameboard
(optional, see Appendix)
4 game tokens:
1 in one color,
3 in a different color**

Difficulty: ● ● ●
Estimated Project Time: 15 minutes

What's the STEAM behind it?

Abstract strategy games have mathematical foundations. Kids are learning about logic, patterning, and sequencing as well as honing their strategy, problem-solving and concentration skills, which are important for science, engineering and technology learning. Kids combine math and art while drawing geometric shapes to create the game board.

Instructions:

1. Create your game board as shown in photo using a ruler, paper and pen. Or print out one of the two game board variations in the Appendix.

2. Place 3 "hound" tokens on the three points at one end.

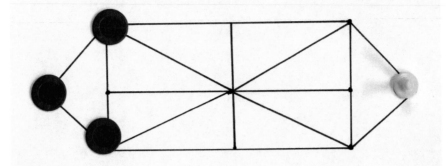

3. The player with the "hare" places him on a point at the far end.

4. The hare's objective is to get past the hounds. The hare can move one point at a time, forward, backward or sideways. He cannot jump over the hounds.

5. The hounds' objective is to trap the hare so that he cannot move. (see photo below for example). The hounds can only move forward or sideways. The hounds cannot move backward and cannot jump over the hare. Only one hound can move per turn.

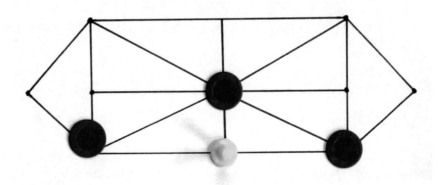

6. Players alternate until either the hare escapes or is trapped by the hounds.

Project Extensions:

● Older kids can try designing new game boards, experimenting with shape and number of lines, and determining their effect on game play. In perfect game play, the hounds will always win; can they figure out what a perfect game would look like? What happens if the hare can start from any point on the game board? Artistic kids can design game tokens to look like a hare and hounds, perhaps even sculpting small tokens.

● Play more abstract strategy games like Five Field Kono from Korea or Dara from Nigeria.

Simple Machine Challenge

Take a stuffie for a ride with this simple machine building challenge

Anne Carey **Left Brain Craft Brain**

Difficulty: ● ● ● ● ●

Estimated Project Time: 1 hour

Materials:

Micscellaneous parts like: wood pieces, buckets, rope, PVC pipe, toys, hula hoops, pool noodles, etc.

Connectors like tape, twist ties, twine

Stuffed animal

What's the STEAM behind it?

This project is a perfect opportunity to learn about simple machines, the building blocks of all things that move.

- **Lever:** A stiff board that rests on a center turning point called a fulcrum that is used to lift objects. Think teeter totter.

- **Wheel and axle:** A wheel with a rod attached to the middle can help lift objects. Think bicycle.

- **Pulley:** Adds a rope to a wheel which allows you to change direction of a force. Think flagpole or window blinds.

- **Inclined plane:** A hard, flat surface with one end higher than the other. Aids in moving objects. Think slide.

- **Wedge:** Two inclined planes put together and helps push objects apart. Think axe.

- **Screw:** An inclined plane wrapped around a pole that can lift objects or hold them together. Think screw.

S T E A M

Instructions:

Your Challenge: Help your favorite stuffed animal travel across the backyard (or your living room) using only simple machines.

1. Grab a favorite stuffed animal, small ones work best.

2. Plan your route and machine design. Some things to think about as you design:

   - Do you need to travel long distances? Wheels make it go faster.

   - Have to go up or down? Pulleys and incline planes can help.

   - Need to break through a tight space? Try a wedge.

3. Build your machines. Use materials that you have or take a trip to the dollar store with your design in mind. There are no wrong ideas in this as the project is about learning from trial and error.

4. Test your machines. If the stuffed animal didn't make it all the way on it's journey, optimize your machines and repeat the test.

Project Extensions:

⬤ For an added challenge, start a design journal to record all ideas, inventions and plans.

⬤ For another simple machine building challenge, try building a Snack Mix Machine.

SENSE

Nature Art Mandala

Create a nature inspired mandala using found objects and preserve it with digital photography.

by Jamie Hand **Handmade Kids Art**

Materials:

Natural objects (rocks, leaves, flowers, twigs, etc)
Digital camera

Difficulty: ● ● ●

Estimated Project Time: 15 minutes

What's the STEAM behind it?

Mandala is an ancient Sanskrit word meaning circle. A circle is a geometric shape that has no beginning or end. Mandala or circular designs are found all throughout nature, from flowers to snowflakes and even the cells in our bodies.

Instructions:

1. Go on a nature walk to collect visually interesting nature objects. Collect objects with a variety of colors, textures and different shapes.

2. Find a clear space on the ground to be your canvas, such as a patch of grass or empty sidewalk. Choose a large size object to be your center starting point.

3. Using your collection of nature objects, form a circle around the center object. Continue to build larger circles around the center object creating a pattern. Challenge yourself to complete five circles.

4. Record your mandala by taking a digital photograph of your work of art.

5. Print out your favorite photograph and frame it to share with family and friends.

Project Extensions:

- Create a permanent mandala by gluing your nature objects to a canvas or try building a mandala with your favorite toys.

- Continue your flower creations with a Digital Flower Still Life.

Bubble Engineering

Engineer the perfect bubble wand for making giant bubbles

Difficulty: ● ● ● ● ●
Estimated Project Time: 20 minutes

What's the STEAM behind it?

Bubbles are formed by the surface tension of water. When you stretch bubbles across your wand, the bubbles cling to the sides as you dip the solution. This allows the bubbles to be all sorts of shapes. Adding soap to your bubble solution reduces the surface tension and slows down the evaporation process, which gives you a long lasting bubble!

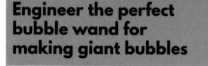

Materials:

Big Bubble Solution:
6 cups water
1/2 cup dish detergent
1/2 cup corn starch
1 tbsp baking powder
1 tbsp glycerine
Containers to hold solution

Materials for Bubble Wands:
Straws
String

by Dayna Abraham **Lemon Lime Adventures**

Instructions:

1. The day before you plan to do this activity, create your big bubble solution. This is simple. Start by mixing the water and cornstarch together until the cornstarch is dissolved. Then add in the other ingredients slowly. Finally, let the mixture thicken until you are ready to create your bubbles.

2. Encourage children to use straws and string to create a bubble wand. There are many ways children can create bubble wands. One simple strategy is to use two straws that are the same length. String your string through the two straws and tie the ends together until you have a square.

3. It is fun to challenge your children to experiment with the number of straws, the length of the string and the size of the straws.

Project Extensions:

● For even bigger bubbles, try hula hoops, hangers, string attached to garden stakes, or bundles of straws.

● Try this Straw Engineering Project for another challenge.

S T E A M

Scent Boxes

Create a sensory scent challenge box

by Amber Scardino **Wee Warhols**

Difficulty: ●

Estimated Project Time: 30 minutes

What's the STEAM behind it?

Our noses are filled with sensory neurons with odor receptors. Substances around us, like flowers or coffee, release molecules that stimulate these neurons. Once the neurons detect the molecules, they send a message to the brain which allows us to identify the smell.

Materials:

**Small jars
Strong smelling items
(i.e. cinnamon, mint,
coffee, fruit peel, etc.)
Blindfold**

Instructions:

1. Put different strong smelling items into various small jars that have a top or cork that traps the smell in the jar. You could also use cotton balls and various extracts to accomplish the same goal.

2. Blind fold the participant. Have them try to guess what scent they are smelling.

Project Extensions:

● Use the scent box to challenge by coming up with games, scavenger hunts, or greater nose challenges. Or decorate the bottles for an art element too.

● Try this Gummy Bear experiment for more sensory science.

S T E A M

Edible Polymer Gummies

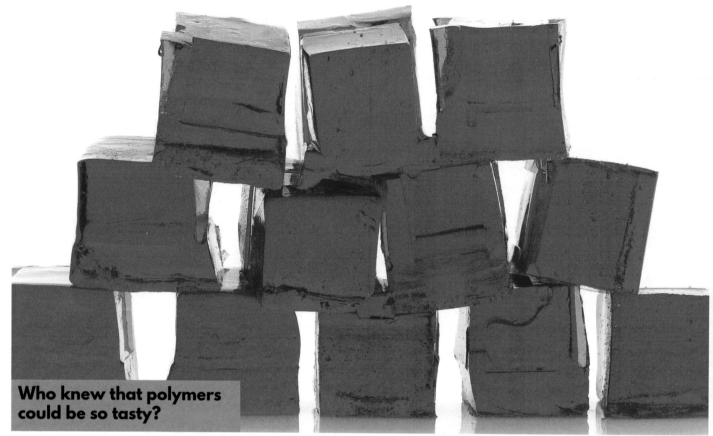

Who knew that polymers could be so tasty?

by Anne Carey **Left Brain Craft Brain**

Materials:

Fruit juice
Unflavored gelatin
Honey (optional)
Pipe cleaners

Difficulty: ● ● ● ●
Estimated Project Time: 20 minutes + chill time

What's the STEAM behind it?

These gummies are made with gelatin, a naturally found protein polymer. When you add the juice to the powdered gelatin, it blooms or swells. Gelatin's proteins form a triple helix (i.e. spiral) polymer chain which allows the food to gel once the molecules in the juice intersperse within the gelatin's helix. Picture it getting bigger like a slinky you've stuffed with tennis balls. The degree of gelling or expansion of the helix, as well as the texture of the gummies depends upon what the gelatin is mixed with. Try mixing with fruit puree for a less jiggly gummy.

Instructions:

Juicy Fruit Gummies

- 2 cups fruit juice

- 4 packets Knox Gelatin (other brands are fine, check package size if using a different brand)

- Honey to taste

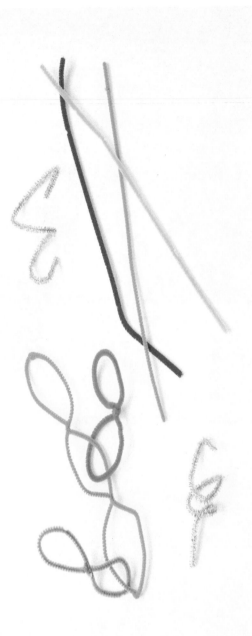

1. Pour 1 1/2 cups of juice into a small sauce pan. Heat over medium heat until it reaches a gentle boil.

2. While juice heats, pour remaining 1/2 cup of juice into a small bowl. Add gelatin and let bloom for five minutes. Discuss polymer chains while blooming.

3. Add gelatin to heated juice and stir until fully dissolved.

4. Take a quick taste of the juice mixture. Is it sweet enough? Add honey and stir until it is.

5. Pour mixture into a 9" square pan. Or use a silicone candy mold (round shapes like hearts work better than pointy shapes like stars).

6. Chill for 1-2 hours and remove from pan or mold. If gummies don't come out easily, chill for another half hour. If using a 9" pan, pull out gummy in one piece by running a knife along edges. Then place on a cutting board and cut into squares of desired size.

7. Store in refrigerator for up to 3-4 days.

Polymer Play

Practice making some polymer chains with pipe cleaners. Can you make a triple helix like gelatin?

Project Extensions:

- Talk about other types of polymers you can find in your house. What do they look like? Did you find any other edible ones? (Think of a chewy one!)

- For more edible science, check out these Play & Learn With Your Food activities.

Symmetry Play Dough

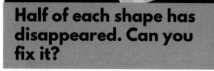

Half of each shape has disappeared. Can you fix it?

by Malia Hollowell **Playdough to Plato**

Difficulty: ●

Estimated Project Time: 20 minutes

What's the STEAM behind it?

The play dough mats teach kids the meaning of "symmetry" (two sides are the same) and stretches their problem solving and visual thinking abilities.

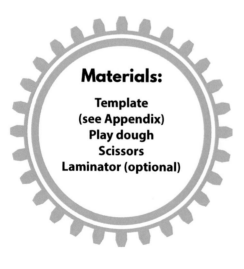

Materials:

Template
(see Appendix)
Play dough
Scissors
Laminator (optional)

Instructions:

1. Print the symmetry play dough mats on cardstock for extra durability.

2. Cut along the black lines to separate them.

3. Laminate the cards for easy reuse.

4. Read the name of the shape on a card and talk about what it looks like.

5. Explain that symmetrical means both halves are the same. Since the shape is symmetrical, the missing side must be the same as the side that is showing.

6. Cover the visible side with play dough.

7. Add playdough to the invisible side to complete the shape.

8. Grab a new card and start again.

Project Extensions:

● For added challenge, draw your own symmetry mats or try building the shapes with LEGO bricks.

● Check out this list for more learning play dough mats.

Sound Spinners

Make a spinning noisemaker toy

by Erica Clark **What Do We Do All Day?**

Difficulty: ●●●●

Estimated Project Time: 30 minutes

What's the STEAM behind it?

The noise is made when the rubber band vibrates against the wooden craft stick. These vibrations create waves in the air that we perceive as sound.

Materials:

Index cards
Markers or crayons
Jumbo craft sticks
Medium width rubber bands
Craft foam
Tape
Scissors
String

Instructions:

1. Decorate and color index cards as desired and tape one card to each side of the craft stick.

2. Cut two strips of craft foam, 4" long by 1/2" wide. Fold strips in half & tape around each end of the craft stick.

3. Stretch rubber band around the length of the craft stick.

4. Cut a length of string 3/4 the length of your arm. Tie string to the craft stick, slipping it under the rubber band.

5. Grasp end of string and spin the noise maker as fast as you can!

Project Extensions:

● What happens if you spin it in different directions, or use different lengths of string?

● Spin art is another unique art & science project.

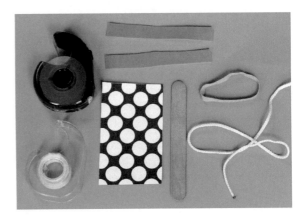

Yummy Comet Frozen Treat

Kids learn about comets in this tasty science activity

by Leslie Manlapig **Pink Stripey Socks**

Materials:

Bananas
(1 banana per serving)
Mix-in items
(ex: cookies, chocolate chips, etc)
Knife
Cutting board
Rolling pin
Blender or food processor
Airtight container
Plastic bag

Difficulty: ●●●●●

Estimated Project Time: several hours

What's the STEAM behind it?

Comets are made up of ice and dust. Here, we are making an edible "comet." The frozen banana represents the ice and the cookies represent the dust. Mix them together to make one delicious cosmic treat!

Instructions:

1. Chop up your bananas into disks.

2. Place your bananas in an airtight freezer container and freeze for 4 hours.

3. Meanwhile, place your mix-in items into a plastic bag. Use a rolling pin (or other heavy object) to crush the items.

4. Place your frozen bananas into a blender or food processor and blend till smooth.

5. Add in your mix-in items.

6. Place your banana mixture into an airtight freezer container and freeze for 4 more hours.

7. Pull out your edible comet and enjoy!

Project Extensions:

- Place your comet frozen treat into a cone to resemble a comet's tail!

- Try this Maple Syrup Snow Candy for another frozen sweet treat.

Pool Noodle Periscope

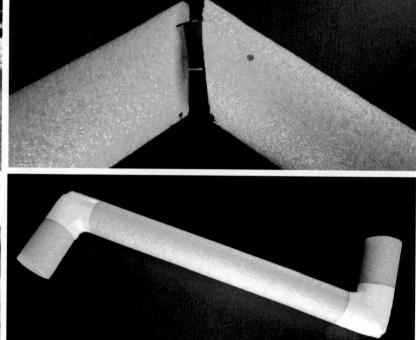

Make your own periscope with leftover pool noodles

by P. R. Newton **STEAM Powered Family**

Difficulty: ● ● ● ●

Estimated Project Time: 30 minutes

What's the STEAM behind it?

The pool noodle periscope is a fun way for kids to explore reflections and to learn a bit about math, measurements and angles. Decorate your periscope to add some art to your project!

Materials:

Pool noodle (a straight one)
Knife or scissors
2 Circular mirrors (diameter shoud be slightly smaller than the pool noodle)
Tape
Protractor
Tape measure
Marker

Instructions:

1. Measure the pool noodle marking 4 inches from the end with a dot, then again at 6 inches from the end with a dot. These will mark the ends of your cuts and results in a 4 inch end piece.

2. Using a protractor mark off a 45 degree angle using the dots as your end points. Cut. Turn and confirm it attaches to form a 90 degree angle. Adjust your cuts until you have a perfect 90 degree angle.

3. Insert the mirror so it dissects the 90 degree corner.

4. Tape your corner together securely.

5. Repeat on the other end but ensure your cuts are reversed so your periscope looks to the front.

Project Extensions:

● For younger children, take tinfoil and wrap it tightly around cardboard to create a reflective surface. This eliminates the need for a mirror which could break if the periscope is handled roughly.

● For older kids, challenge them to make periscopes that look behind them.

S T E A M

Gelatin Science

Learn about light refraction and reflection with this jiggly experiment

by Karyn Tripp **Teach Beside Me**

Difficulty: ●●

Estimated Project Time: 20 minutes + gelatin set time

What's the STEAM behind it?

Science is used in making the gelatin as well as the reflecting and refracting of light within the gelatin. Add math to the mix by measuring the refraction angles of light through the gelatin.

Materials:

**1 box of plain gelatin
laser pointer
small mirror**

Instructions:

1. Prepare Gelatin according to package directions and pour the into a greased pan. Chill until hardened.

2. Remove hardened gelatin from pan and place on a tray where the gelatin edges can be reached.

3. Use a laser pointer and point it through the gelatin. (For maximum effect, try this in a dark room!) See how far it will go through before the light dies.

4. Using a mirror try reflecting the light back through the gelatin. It works well on the corners.

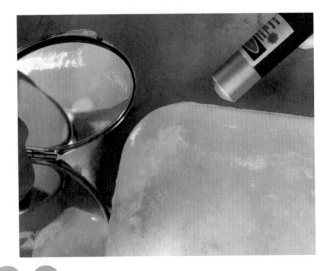

Project Extensions:

● Measure the changes in light refraction angles when reflecting the light with mirrors, break the gelatin into pieces or change the color of light.

● Try this <u>Gelatin Science & Art Project</u> too!

S T E A M

Homemade Drums

Explore the science of sound with homemade drums

by Chelsey Marashian **Buggy and Buddy**

Materials:

Containers for body of drum:
oatmeal canister, shoebox,
tin can etc.
Materials for top of drum:
wax paper, plastic wrap, fabric,
newspaper etc.
Rubber bands
Tape
Scissors
Craft supplies (optional)
Decibel meter or app

Difficulty: ● ● ●

Estimated Project Time: 30 minutes

What's the STEAM behind it?

Children explore the science of sound by building their very own drums. The use of a decibel meter incorporates the importance of technology in building and engineering, as well as demonstrating the importance of math as numbers are compared. Art can be used to personalize the homemade drums!

S T E A M

Instructions:

1. Start by building a drum made from any of the materials you've gathered. Select a container to use for the body of the drum and a material to use for the top. Attach the material to the top of your container securely using a rubber band or tape. Use your hand to beat on the drum. How does it sound?

2. Set a decibel meter near the drum. How high can you get your meter to go using your homemade drum? Record your result.

3. Try altering the drum or building a whole new drum. Test how loud your new drum is using the decibel meter.

4. Which combinations of materials make the loudest sound? The quietest? Why do you think different materials and containers affect the drum sound?

5. Optional: Select your favorite drum combination and decorate the final drum using paints and craft supplies. Use it to make your own music!

Project Extensions:

- Create a chart on paper or on a computer to record your data. Try this same activity with other homemade instruments like guitars or rainsticks!

- Create a whole band with these DIY Kazoos, too.

GROW

Rainbow Diaper Science

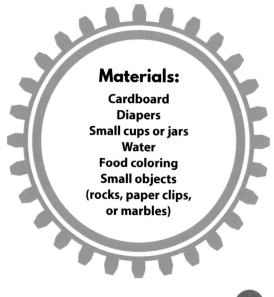

Explore the magic absorbing power of diapers in this experiment

by Dayna Abraham **Lemon Lime Adventures**

Difficulty: ●

Estimated Project Time: 30 minutes

What's the STEAM behind it?

Diapers contain a super-absorbing polymer called Sodium Polyacrylate. While many polymers are hydrophobic (repels water), polyacrylic acid is hydrophillic (attracts water). This polymer can absorb up to 800 times its own weight in water. The "growing" you are seeing is the polymer chains linking together and attracting the water.

Materials:

Cardboard
Diapers
Small cups or jars
Water
Food coloring
Small objects
(rocks, paper clips, or marbles)

Instructions:

1. Begin by opening a clean diaper and lying it flat over a paper or plastic container.

2. Have an adult cut open the diaper in the center to expose the fluff and powder.

3. Collect the "powder" from a few diapers and pour into your jars.

4. After making predictions and observations, pour water colored by food coloring into the jars.

5. Watch as the powder starts to absorb the water and grow to fill or overflow from the jars.

6. Don't stop there! Experiment with different brand diapers, different ratios of water to powder, and different size containers. Curious how dense your new gel is? Try to drop various small objects in the jar and see if it sinks or floats. Try mixing colors, too.

Project Extensions:

● Using the newly color diaper jelly, create art jars much like sand art. For more science, try these <u>sensory bottles</u> that explore absorption.

S T E A M

Rock Candy Geodes

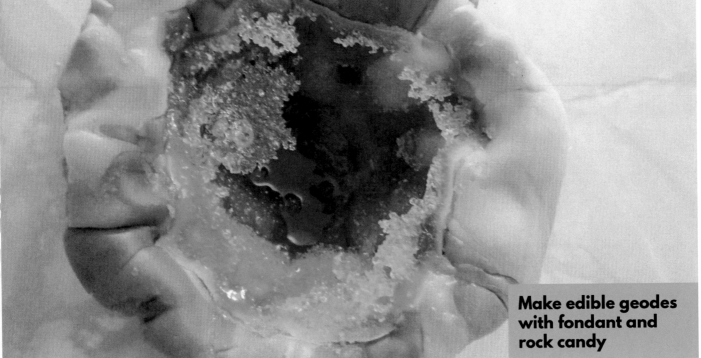

Make edible geodes with fondant and rock candy

by Karyn Tripp **Teach Beside Me**

Difficulty: ● ● ●

Estimated Project Time: 3-5 days

What's the STEAM behind it?

The sugar crystals in these edible rocks form in similar ways to actual geodes as liquids evaporate and leave behind the mineral crystals.

Materials:

Fondant
Sugar
Gel food coloring
Bowls
Foil

Instructions:

1. Color the fondant to look like rocks with black and brown food coloring. Leave it marbled for a realistic effect.

2. Line a small bowl (1 per geode) with foil. Roll the fondant out and layer it over the foil.

3. Make a sugar syrup for the geode by mixing 1 c. water and 2 c. white sugar. Heat over medium heat in a small pot until dissolved. Add in food coloring and pour the sugar syrup into the hollow of the fondant rock.

4. Wrap the entire bowl in foil and seal it up. Let it set for about three days. The sugar will crystalize. You can open it and peek, but watch out for spilling! It get's messy. After three days, pour out the extra liquid and let it dry opened.

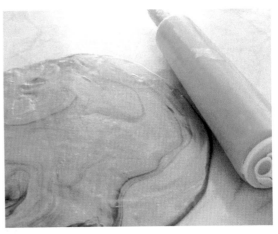

Project Extensions:

● For more fun, make homemade fondant with this recipe.

S **T** **E** **A** **M**

Growing Seeds Science

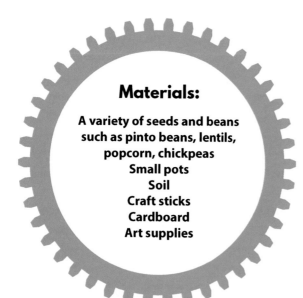

Watch how different types of seeds grow using common kitchen pantry items

by Erica Clark **What Do We Do All Day?**

Materials:

A variety of seeds and beans such as pinto beans, lentils, popcorn, chickpeas
Small pots
Soil
Craft sticks
Cardboard
Art supplies

Difficulty: ● ●

Estimated Project Time: 1-3 weeks

What's the STEAM behind it?

Kids will learn about plant science as they watch seeds and beans they normally eat produce sprouts. They can discuss the speed at which the different seeds grow, and when they dig up the sprouts they can observe how the sprout emerges from the seed.

S T E A M

Instructions:

1. Design and make plant markers by gluing cardboard to craft sticks and decorating.

2. Label each marker with the name of the seeds.

3. Fill pots 3/4 full with soil.

4. Place seeds in soil, about 1/2 inch down.

5. Insert plant markers into pots, as appropriate

6. Place in sunny window and water.

7. Keep soil moist until seedlings sprout.

8. After seeds sprout, unearth several of them to observe how the sprout emerged from the seed.

Project Extensions:

- For an added challenge, design and plan an outdoor vegetable garden or try Regrowing Vegetables from Scraps. Experiment with different types of scraps like lettuce, avocado pits, or parsnips and record your observations. Which types of vegetables regrow more readily? What part of the plant do you need in order to promote growth?

Mama Succulent Leaf

Learn about how plants multiply with this propogation experiment

by Amber Scardino **Wee Warhols**

Difficulty: ● ● ●

Estimated Project Time: 1 week

What's the STEAM behind it?

Propagation is the process of creating new plants. Some plants use seeds and bulbs, but some can be grown through cuttings of leaves and stems. This experiment shows how new leaves can sprout from an older leaf that has been removed from the stem.

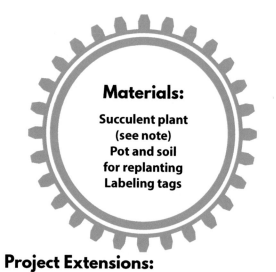

Materials:

**Succulent plant (see note)
Pot and soil for replanting
Labeling tags**

Project Extensions:

● Older kids can expand the project by researching other plants that also produce baby plants externally. Or for another plant activity, try these Valentine Succulent Terrariums.

Instructions:

Note: Choose a succulent plant that has become leggy, a plant having an excessively long and straggly stem. Baby Blue Kalanchoe succulent leaves work well. Not all varieties of succulents will produce new plants, so be sure to ask a plant nursery if you're unsure.

1. Gently remove the leaves from the bottom of the plant by wiggling them side to side, careful to retain the base of the leaf. You could also use a leaf that has fallen.

2. Label cutting with dated tags, so the kids can keep track of the start and the end of the project.

3. Let the cutting sit out in a warm, dry place with indirect sunlight. To replant this leaf, let the end of the stem callus dry before planting it. Otherwise, if replanted right away they will absorb too much moisture and rot.)

4. After a 5-7 days, roots will sprout from the ends of the leaves, then little baby plants will grow.

5. When you feel like the "parent" leaf has given it's all and withers, remove it carefully, keeping the new roots intact. Replant the babies in well-draining soil. Be sure not to overwater and avoid placing new plants in direct sunlight.

S T E A M

3-D Puffy Paint

by Jamie Hand **Handmade Kids Art**

Difficulty: ● ●

Estimated Project Time: 15 minutes

What's the STEAM behind it?

Baking powder is a chemical leavening agent which causes batter to rise when baked. Many types of baking powder are "double acting." The first reaction occurs when you mix the baking powder with a liquid and carbon dioxide is released causing bubbles. A second reaction takes place when heat is applied to the baking powder.

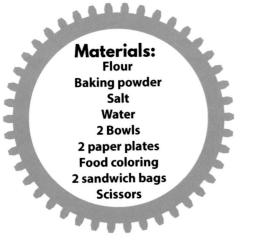

Materials:
Flour
Baking powder
Salt
Water
2 Bowls
2 paper plates
Food coloring
2 sandwich bags
Scissors

Project Extensions:

● Create your own puffy paint recipe. What happens if you add more or less baking powder to the recipe?

Instructions:

1. In one bowl mix 1 cup of flour, three teaspoons of baking powder and one teaspoon of salt. Slowly add water to the mix and stir until you have the consistency similar to pancake batter. In the second bowl, repeat the same process but omit the baking powder. Once again match your mix to the consistency of pancake batter.

2. Spoon the mixture from your first bowl into a plastic sandwich bag. Add 5-7 drops of food coloring. Seal the bag and mix the color around until the mixture is evenly colored. Cut one corner tip of the plastic bag. Squeeze the paint onto a paper plate to create your painted design. Repeat as needed for additional colors.

3. Repeat step 2 with your mixture from the second bowl on a different paper plate. Compare the plates and predict what you think will happen once the paint is heated in the microwave.

4. Place each plate in the microwave for 45 seconds. Compare the heated designs. What is different about the painted plates?

Fun with Fungus

Watch the wonder of fungus grow in this easy science experiment.

by Anne Carey **Left Brain Craft Brain**

Materials:
Petri dishes
2 1/2 tsp. sugar
2 1/2 tsp. agar powder
2 Cups beef broth
2 Cups water
Q-tips
Zipper bags
Bread or other
food that molds

Difficulty: ● ● ● ●
Estimated Project Time: 4 to 5 days

What's the STEAM behind it?

Fungi are a group of organisms called eukaryotes that include single cell organisms like yeasts and mold. Multi-cell organisms like mushrooms are also a type of fungus. They have their own kingdom, along with plants, animals, protists and bacteria due their their unique cell structure. Fungi have five characteristics that separate them from the other kingdoms:

- Their cells contain nuclei like plants and animals.
- They can't photosynthesize like plants can.
- They absorb their food instead of making their own.
- Multi-cellular fungi grow via networks of long tubular filaments called hyphae.
- They usually reproduce via spores.

86

Instructions:

SAFETY NOTE: Wash your hands after handling fungus sample petri dishes and never touch the samples directly with your hands. A mask or other breathing protection is also recommended as breathing the spores can be dangerous.

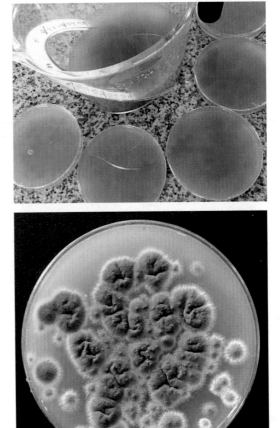

Make the Agar Plates

1. Pour the beef broth and water into a pan. Bring to a boil.

2. Add sugar and agar powder and stir over medium heat until dissolved.

3. Pour into petri dishes. Cool in refrigerator until hardened.

Test for Mold

4. Using a Q-tip, swipe across any surface that you want to test for mold. Then swipe Q-tip across a hardened agar plate. Be sure to use only one test area per petri dish.

5. Cover petri dish and place inside a zipper bag. Store in a warm dark place until mold grows, approximately 4-5 days.

6. How many different types of fungus can you see on your samples?

Explore Food Mold
Grab your favorite food and let it sit in a zipper bag until fungus grows. Does it look the same as the samples you gathered with the Q-tips?

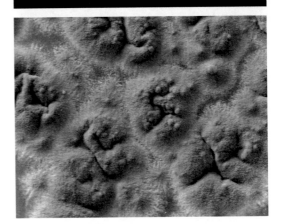

Make Fungus Art
Once you know what color the fungus is, you can take a Q-tip sample and decorate your petri dish in a colorful pattern.

Project Extensions:

● As an extension to this fungi experiment, investigate the other five Kingdoms: Plants, Animals, Archaebacteria, Eubacteria, and Protists. Make a batch of <u>Homemade Yogurt</u> to learn about the beneficial bacteria in that delicious food.

Crazy Monster Pet

Difficulty: ● ●

Estimated Project Time: 30 minutes + grow time

What's the STEAM behind it?

Plants need dirt, sun and water to grow. When seeds begin to sprout, they grow roots that stretch down in the dirt to collect water below. The sprout stems grow up to gather more sunlight which they absorb to create "plant food" through a process called photosynthesis.

Materials:
Clear plastic cup
Dirt
Packet of fast sprouting seeds
(grass, spinach, chives, etc.)
Scissors
Hot glue gun
Colored paper
Optional:
Miniature pom poms
Googly eyes
Cheerios

by Malia Hollowell **Playdough to Plato**

Instructions:

1. Fill the cup with dirt, leaving 1/2 inch of space at the top. Use your pointer finger to poke holes in the dirt. Read the back of your seed packet to determine how deep each hole should be.

2. Drop one seed in each hole and cover it with dirt.

3. Place the cup in a sunny windowsill and water the seeds according to the directions on the packet.

4. While the sprouts grow, create your monster. Cut out a monster face that is large enough to cover your cup. Decorate the face with googly eyes, paper circles, Cheerios, miniature pom poms... anything you can imagine!

5. Glue the monster face to the side of your cup to make a sprout monster.

Project Extensions:

● Test the plant cycle by changing one plant's light and water supply. Did it grow the same? Or try one of these other Plant Life Cycle projects.

S T E A M

Growing Shadow Artwork

Explore how shadows change throughout the day with this unique art project.

by Leslie Manlapig **Pink Stripey Socks**

Difficulty: ●

Estimated Project Time: several hours

What's the STEAM behind it?

The toys cast shadows by blocking the sunlight. As the day progresses, their shadows change. They grow and shrink according to the sun's position in the sky.

Materials:
Paper
Toys
Tape
Markers

Instructions:

1. Tape a piece of paper to the ground.

2. Place toys on your paper. Tape them down if it's a windy day.

3. Starting from early morning, trace the toys' shadows once every hour.

4. Observe what happens to the shadows as the day progresses.

Project Extensions:

● Repeat this activity over several days. Note what happens to the shadows! Or, color in your shadow silhouettes with watercolors or markers.

● For more fun in the sun, try these Sun Prints.

S T E A M

Crystal Landscapes

Learn how to grow colorful DIY Crystal Landscapes using salt and bluing

by Ana Dziengel **Babble Dabble Do**

Materials:

2 Bottles of bluing
(available at a hardware store or online)
Salt
Water
Ammonia
Large tray or cookie sheet with sides
Sponges
Scissors
Measuring cup
Liquid watercolors or
Food coloring
Eye droppers

Difficulty: ● ● ● ● ●

Estimated Project Time: 4 to 5 days

What's the STEAM behind it?

Crystals are groups of molecules bonded together in repetitive patterns. Crystals form through a process called crystallization in which a supersaturated liquid solution is allowed to evaporate and certain molecules in the solution begin to bond together during evaporation. In this project, the salt forms crystals on the sponges as the water evaporates. The ammonia helps speed up the process and the bluing (a powder used to keep laundry white) transforms the crystals into blooms instead of more geometric shaped crystals.

S T E A M

Instructions:

Day One

1. Cut sponges into chunks. Spread them around your tray.

2. Measure out 1 cup of each of the following: salt, water, bluing. Sprinkle the ingredients over the sponges in this order: ½ salt, ½ water, all the bluing, ½ salt, ½ water.

Day Two

3. Add 1 cup of ammonia and sprinkle an additional cup of salt over the sponges.

Day Three

4. Sprinkle 1 cup of each of the following onto your garden: salt, bluing, water. Pour as much of the ingredients as possible into the pan rather than directly on top of the crystals.

5. Using an eyedropper drop a tablespoon of each color of undiluted liquid watercolor or food coloring on the sponges/crystals.

Days Four & Five

6. Observe the crystal growth. Over the course of a few days the crystals should be larger and less vibrant as the coloring dissipates.

7. You may keep your landscape growing indefinitely by adding small amounts of water, bluing and salt every few days.

TIPS

- Allow for plenty of air circulation to foster the crystal growth.

- Grow these inside! Cool nighttime air will inhibit crystal growth.

- Ammonia is not necessary but speeds up the evaporation and crystal growth. You can purchase it at your local hardware store with the cleaning supplies. Take precautions with it as it is an irritant.

Project Extensions:

- Remove a sample of the crystals and observe them under a microscope.

- Experiment with the crystal growth by growing a batch without ammonia and another batch without bluing. How does this affect the crystal growth both in timing and form?

- Try growing crystals on different substrates. Ideas to try: charcoal, toilet paper rolls, cardboard cut in the shape of trees, etc.

- For fast growing crystals, try these Overnight Crystal Gardens.

ACTIVITY PLANNER

Have a summer camp to plan?
Or need activities for spring break?
Maybe it's Family STEAM Night at school.
We've planned it for you!
The next 11 pages provide week-long
activity guides and shopping lists to make
those hands-on learning opportunities
easy for you.

Week 1 Projects

Build: Mud Bricks
Play: Bottle Rockets
Color: Color Changing Play Dough
Grow: Crystal Landscape
Sense: Comet Frozen Treat

Materials List

- dirt
- water
- bowl
- spoon
- ice cube tray
- plastic 2L bottles
- vinegar
- baking soda
- paper towels
- cork

- building blocks
- craft supplies
- flour
- salt
- cream of tartar
- thermochromic pigment
- vegetable oil
- liqud watercolors or food coloring

- bluing
- ammonia
- tray or cookie sheet
- sponges
- scissors
- measuring cup
- eye droppers
- airtight container
- plastic bag

- bananas
- mix-in items: cookies, chocolate chips, etc.
- knife
- cutting board
- rolling pin
- blender or food processor

Week 2 Projects

Build: Clay & Block Structures
Play: Stop Motion Video
Color: Oil & Watercolors
Grow: Rock Candy Geodes
Sense: Sound Spinners

<u>Materials List</u>

- air dry clay
- toy wooden blocks
- LEGO Minifigures or dolls, clay figures, cars, toys
- thick paper or
- foamcore
- smart phone or table
- Flipagram app

- cookie sheet
- watercolor paper
- liquid watercolors or food coloring
- bowls
- eye droppers or pipettes
- cooking oil
- paper towels

- fondant
- sugar
- gel food coloring
- bowls
- foil
- markers or crayons
- jumbo craft sticks
- rubber bands
- index cards

- craft foam
- tape
- scissors
- string

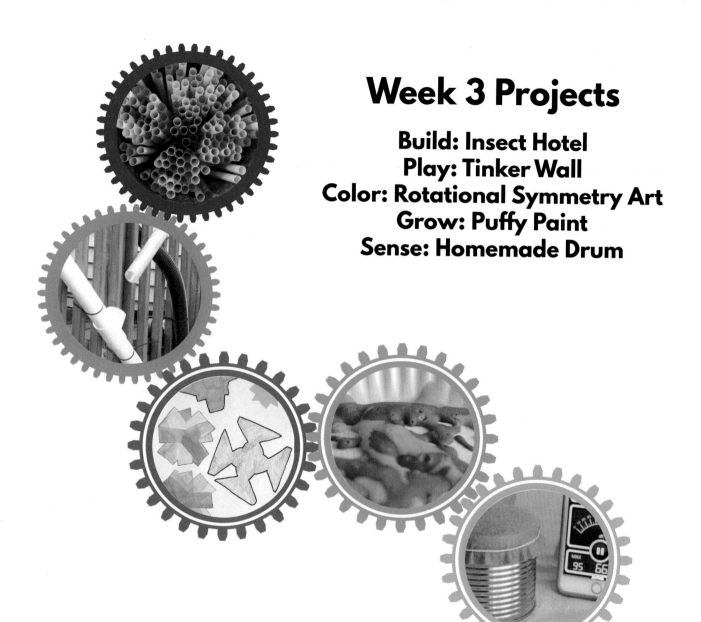

Week 3 Projects

Build: Insect Hotel
Play: Tinker Wall
Color: Rotational Symmetry Art
Grow: Puffy Paint
Sense: Homemade Drum

Materials List

- clay pot
- aluminum foil
- wax
- smoothie straws
- twine
- flour
- baking powder
- salt
- water
- bowls

- paper plates
- food coloring
- sandwich bags
- scissors
- paper
- pencil
- push pins
- cardboard
- art supplies

- tubes
- gutters
- twist ties
- PVC pipes
- buckets
- balls
- water balloons
- timer (optional)
- rubber bands
- tape

- drum containers: oatmeal canister, shoebox, tin can
- drum materials: wax paper, plastic wrap, fabric, newspaper
- decibel meter or app

Week 4 Projects

Build: Building Challenge
Play: Bubble Trays
Color: Glow Stick Light Painting
Grow: Fun with Fungus
Sense: Pool Noodle Periscope

Materials List

- building supports and connections (see appendix for full list)
- paper
- pencil
- ruler
- timer
- bubble solution
- tray

- straws
- camera or smart phone
- tripod
- glow sticks
- petri dishes
- sugar
- agar powder
- beef broth
- water

- Q-tips
- zipper bags
- bread
- pool noodle
- knife or scissors
- round mirrors
- tape
- protractor
- tape measure
- marker

Week 5 Projects

Build: Toy Car Marker Bots
Play: Pendulum Painting
Color: Prism Play
Grow: Crazy Monster Pets
Sense: Bubble Engineering

Materials List

- Hot Wheels race cars
- skinny washable marker
- 1.5V hobby motor
- dime
- electrical tape
- AAA battery
- wire
- craft or art paper

- glue gun
- Styrofoam cup
- string
- scissors
- pencil
- tape
- 2 chairs
- broom
- paint
- prisms

- patterned paper
- clear plastic cup
- dirt
- fast sprouting seeds (grass, spinach, chives, etc.)
- colored paper
- miniature pom poms
- googly eyes

- Cheerios
- water
- dish soap
- corn starch
- baking powder
- glycerine
- containers to hold bubble solution
- straws
- string

Week 6 Projects

Build: PVC Pipe Slingshot
Play: Ice Cream Roll & Color Game
Color: Graffiti Art
Grow: Rainbow Diaper Science
Sense: Nature Mandalas

Materials List

- 1/2" Schedule 40 PVC pipe
- PVC fittings (no threads):
- 1 x 1/2"T-shaped joint
- 2 x 90-degree 1/2" elbow joints
- 2 x 1/2" caps
- PVC cement
- 17" rubber bands
- small zip ties

- 2 cup round food storage bowl
- drawer knob with screw
- metal washers duct tape
- water balloons
- tape measure
- scissors
- natural objects (rocks, leaves, flowers, twigs, etc.)
- digital camera

- sharp blade
- drill with small bit
- handsaw
- paper
- dice
- crayons
- large wooden frame or large embroidery hoop
- staple gun
- white cotton bed sheet
- water

- food coloring or liquid watercolors
- rubbing alcohol (70%-90%)
- Sharpies
- large paintbrushes
- disposable pipettes
- cardboard
- disposable diapers
- small cups or jars
- found items: (rocks, paper clips, marbles)

Week 7 Projects

**Build: Egg Drop Challenge
Play: Candy Maze
Color: Bleeding Blossoms
Grow: Seed Science
Sense: Gelatin Science**

Materials List

- raw egg
- recyclables: (shoe box, newspaper, egg carton, cardboard tubes, straws, etc.)
- tape
- string
- glue
- art supplies
- gummy candies

- round hard candy
- Styrofoam tray
- tooth picks
- scissors
- paper
- printer
- water soluble markers
- 6" bamboo skewer
- paper towel
- wood bead

- cup
- spray bottle with water
- seeds and beans: (pinto beans, lentils, popcorn, chickpeas)
- small pots
- soil
- craft sticks
- cardboard

- 1 box of plain gelatin
- laser pointer
- small mirror

Week 8 Projects

Build: Paper Circuits
Play: Ribbon Rocket
Color: Milk Plastic Bracelets
Grow: Shadow Artwork
Sense: Scent Boxes

Materials List

- copper tape (peel & stick)
- 3 volt coin battery-size: CR 2032
- small LED light
- small binder clip
- index cards, or other card stock
- pencil
- scissors

- art supplies
- toilet paper rolls
- curling gift ribbon
- paint
- colored paper
- bowl
- spoon
- 2% milk
- white vinegar or lemon juice

- stove top or microwave
- strainer or cheesecloth
- paper towel
- silicone molds or bubble tea straws
- stretchy jewelry cord
- paper

- toys
- tape
- markers
- small jars or boxes
- strong smelling items (i.e. cinnamon, mint, coffee, fruit peel, etc.)
- blind fold

Week 9 Projects

Build: Circuit Bugs
Play: Simple Machine Challenge
Color: Rainbow Reactions
Grow: Mama Succulent Leaf
Sense: Symmetry Play Dough

Materials List

- 2 LED bulbs
- insulated copper magnet wire
- batteries: CR2032 3V
- electrical tape
- clothespins
- popsicle sticks
- succulent plant pot
- soil

- labeling tags
- miscellaneous parts: (wood pieces, buckets, rope, PVC pipe, toys, hula hoops, pool noodles, etc.)
- connectors: (tape, twist ties, twine)
- stuffed animal

- cardboard
- twist ties
- small plastic cups
- large plastic cups
- baking soda
- vinegar
- food coloring gel
- OPTIONAL:
- white paper or canvas

- coffee stirrers
- paper
- play dough
- scissors
- laminator
- dish soap

Week 10 Projects

Build: Craft Stick Catapult
Play: If-Then Coding Game
Color: 3-D Color Wheel
Play: Hare & Hound Game
Sense: Edible Polymers

Materials List

- craft sticks
- rubber bands
- hot glue gun
- bottle lid
- soft object to launch: (pom poms, marshmallows, etc.)
- thin white paper plates
- paint

- paint brushes
- paper clips
- paper
- pen
- ruler
- 4 game tokens: 1 in one color, 3 in a different color
- fruit juice
- unflavored gelatin

- honey (optional)
- pipe cleaners

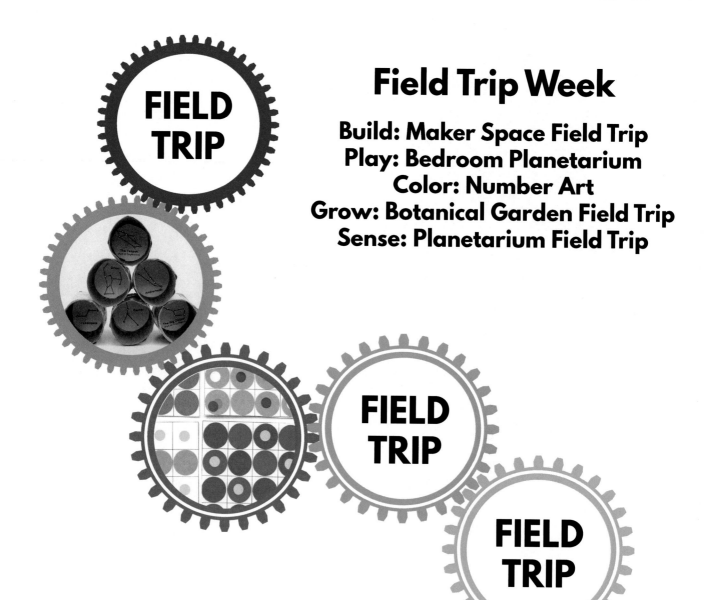

Field Trip Week

Build: Maker Space Field Trip
Play: Bedroom Planetarium
Color: Number Art
Grow: Botanical Garden Field Trip
Sense: Planetarium Field Trip

Materials List

- paper
- printer
- tape
- flashlight (or smart-phone flashlight)
- cardstock
- toilet paper rolls
- scissors
- duct tape
- pins & toothpick
- circle stickers
- 8 1/2" x 11" paper
- pen or pencil

STEAM Field Trip Ideas

STEAM is all around us! Explore physics while having fun playing. Learn about biology while exploring a farm or food. Discover what makes color work while mixing them at an art studio. Use your imagination to find new ways to discover STEAM or use this list for ideas.

BUILD

maker space
LEGO store
sculpture garden
construction site
pipeworks / waterworks
historical buildings
quarry
hardware store

PLAY

science museum
children's museum
park / playground
climbing gym
parkour gym
skate park
amusement park
space museum

COLOR

art store
art museum
craft store
color run
forests in different seasons
rose gardens
pottery painting
art studio

GROW

botanical garden
park
national parks
conservatories
plant nursery
geology museum
rock collecting outing
farm

SENSE

planetarium
grocery store / farmers market
food factory
music concerts
zoo or petting zoo
drum circle
beach or sand pit
perfumery

APPENDIX

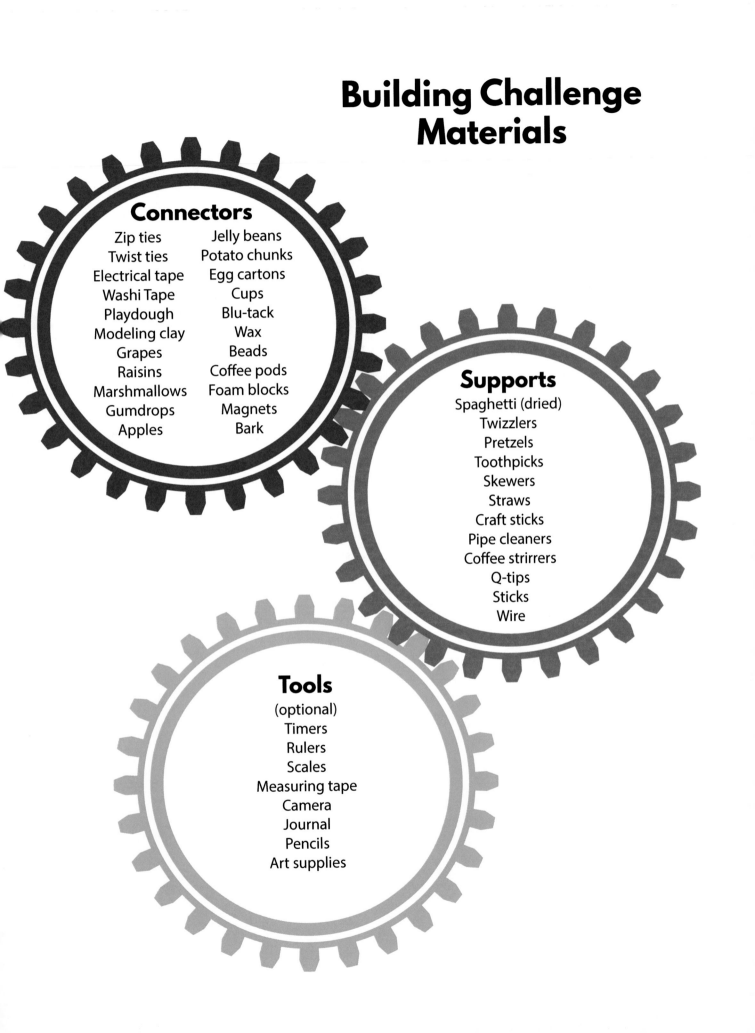

Building Challenge Materials

Connectors

Zip ties
Twist ties
Electrical tape
Washi Tape
Playdough
Modeling clay
Grapes
Raisins
Marshmallows
Gumdrops
Apples
Jelly beans
Potato chunks
Egg cartons
Cups
Blu-tack
Wax
Beads
Coffee pods
Foam blocks
Magnets
Bark

Supports

Spaghetti (dried)
Twizzlers
Pretzels
Toothpicks
Skewers
Straws
Craft sticks
Pipe cleaners
Coffee stirrers
Q-tips
Sticks
Wire

Tools

(optional)
Timers
Rulers
Scales
Measuring tape
Camera
Journal
Pencils
Art supplies

1	2	3	4	5
6	7	8	9	10
11	12	13	14	15
16	17	18	19	20
21	22	23	24	25

1	2	3	4	5
6	7	8	9	10
11	12	13	14	15
16	17	18	19	20
21	22	23	24	25

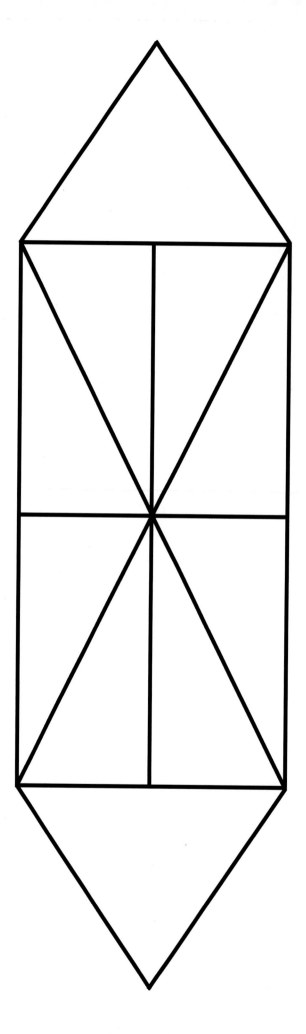

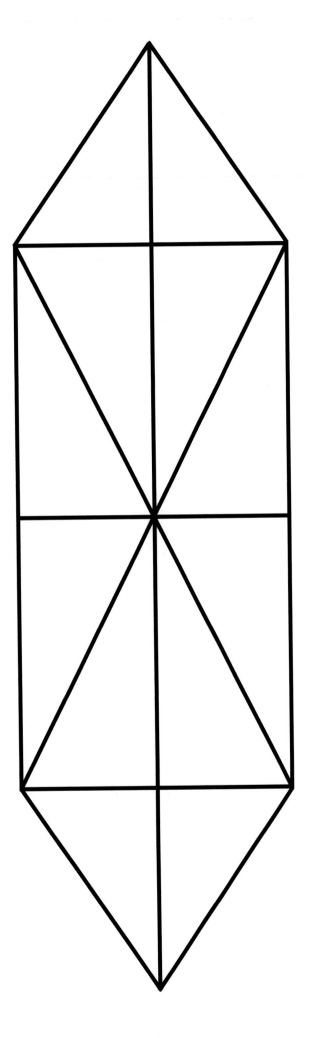

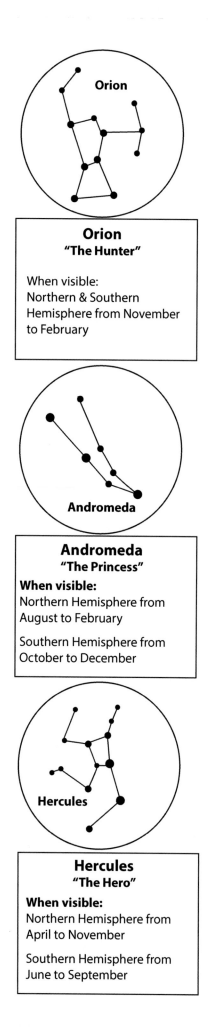

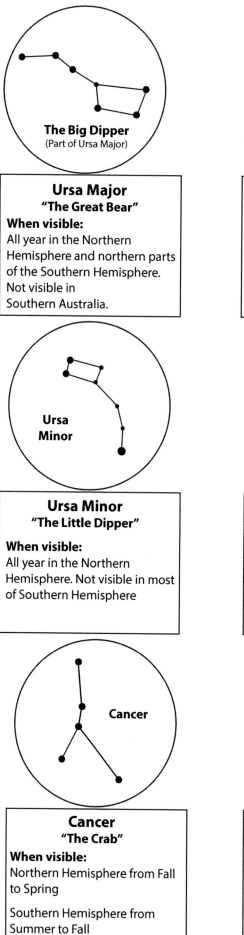

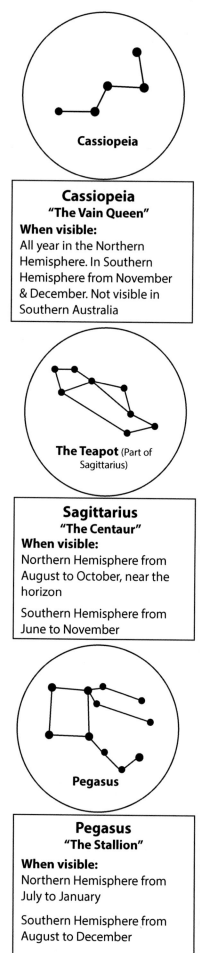

Orion
"The Hunter"

When visible:
Northern & Southern
Hemisphere from November
to February

Ursa Major
"The Great Bear"
When visible:
All year in the Northern
Hemisphere and northern parts
of the Southern Hemisphere.
Not visible in
Southern Australia.

Cassiopeia
"The Vain Queen"
When visible:
All year in the Northern
Hemisphere. In Southern
Hemisphere from November
& December. Not visible in
Southern Australia

Andromeda
"The Princess"
When visible:
Northern Hemisphere from
August to February

Southern Hemisphere from
October to December

Ursa Minor
"The Little Dipper"
When visible:
All year in the Northern
Hemisphere. Not visible in most
of Southern Hemisphere

Sagittarius
"The Centaur"
When visible:
Northern Hemisphere from
August to October, near the
horizon

Southern Hemisphere from
June to November

Hercules
"The Hero"
When visible:
Northern Hemisphere from
April to November

Southern Hemisphere from
June to September

Cancer
"The Crab"
When visible:
Northern Hemisphere from Fall
to Spring

Southern Hemisphere from
Summer to Fall

Pegasus
"The Stallion"
When visible:
Northern Hemisphere from
July to January

Southern Hemisphere from
August to December

Name _____

ice cream color up

Roll one die. Read the number that lands on top. Color it below. Continue rolling and coloring until all ice cream cones have been filled.

Name _____

ice cream color up

Roll two dice. Add together the numbers that land on top. Color the sum below. Continue rolling and coloring until all ice cream cones have been filled.

Name. _____

ice cream color up

Roll three dice. Add together the numbers that land on top. Color the sum below. Continue rolling and coloring until all ice cream cones have been filled.

OVAL

HEXAGON

HEART

CIRCLE

OCTAGON

RHOMBUS

© Playdough to Plato.

TRIANGLE

TRAPEZOID

SQUARE

RECTANGLE

STAR

PENTAGON

50+ More Hands-On STEAM Activities to Try

Like what you found in BUILD, COLOR, PLAY, SENSE & GROW?

Check out these extension projects that keep curious minds growing.

(These are the extensions projects mentioned at the bottom of the projects in the rest of the book.)

Extension projects for activities found in the **BUILD** chapter:

BUILD

1. **Pitfall Insect Trap:** http://teachbesideme.com/pitfall-insect-trap/

2. **Brush Bots:** http://leftbraincraftbrain.com/2015/05/27/minion-brush-bots/

3. **Paper Plate Marble Maze:** http://buggyandbuddy.com/paper-plate-marble-maze/

4. **Travel Engineering Kit:** http://lemonlimeadventures.com/building-with-playdough-simple-stem-challenge-for-kids/

5. **Building with Straws:** http://lemonlimeadventures.com/building-with-straws-engineering-challenge-for-kids/

6. **PVC Pipe Construction Projects:** http://www.weewarhols.com/pvc-pipe-construction-wee-warhols/

7. **Circuit Trees:** http://www.steampoweredfamily.com/activities/circuit-tree-a-steam-activity/

8. **Squishy Circuit Jack 'o-Lantern:** http://www.steampoweredfamily.com/activities/halloween-pumpkins-with-squishy-circuits/

9. **Aluminum Foil Circuits:** http://www.whatdowedoallday.com/2015/03/simple-circuit-science-project.html

10. **Stixplosions:** http://babbledabbledo.com/steam-activity-stixplosions/

11. **100 Invitations to Build:** http://leftbraincraftbrain.com/2016/03/15/100-invitations-build-iggy-peck-architect/

12. **Preschool Engineering:** http://handmadekidsart.com/invitation-build-preschool-stem-activities/

Extension projects for activities found in the **COLOR** chapter:

1. **Rainbow Reactions:** http://lemonlimeadventures.com/rainbow-reactions/
2. **Pi Day Activities:** http://www.pinkstripeysocks.com/search/label/Pi%20dayi
3. **Paper Marbling:** http://www.weewarhols.com/paper-marbling-with-kids/
4. **Color Changing Slime:** http://leftbraincraftbrain.com/2015/04/23/heat-sensitive-color-changing-slime/
5. **Oil Pastels & Watercolors Science Project:** http://leftbraincraftbrain.com/2016/01/04/art-equals-science-paint-solubility-project-kids/
6. **Glow Stick Engineering:** http://handmadekidsart.com/glow-stick-engineering-for-kids/
7. **Milk Plastic Project Extensions:** http://www.steampoweredfamily.com/activities/make-plastic-from-milk/
8. **Math Art Projects:** http://www.whatdowedoallday.com/2014/05/math-art-projects-kids.html
9. **Light Pattern Box:** http://buggyandbuddy.com/reflection-science-with-light-patterns-in-a-box/
10. **Kirigami Water Blossoms:** http://babbledabbledo.com/science-for-kids-kirigami-water-blossoms/
11. **Walking Water:** http://teachbesideme.com/rainbow-science-absorption/

Extension projects for activities found in the **PLAY** chapter:

1. **Bubble Patterns:** http://buggyandbuddy.com/exploring-bubble-patterns/
2. **Straw Rockets:** http://teachbesideme.com/straw-rocket-with-printable-template/
3. **Constellation Geoboards:** http://babbledabbledo.com/constellation-geoboards/
4. **Ice Cream in a Bag:** http://www.playdoughtoplato.com/kids-science-ice-cream-in-a-bag/
5. **LEGO Marble Maze:** http://lemonlimeadventures.com/lego-marble-maze-for-valentines-day/
6. **Gravity Painting:** http://artfulparent.com/2015/03/gravity-painting-a-steam-art-project-for-kids.html
7. **Coding Games for Kids:** http://leftbraincraftbrain.com/2016/02/29/coding-for-kids/
8. **Hatching Dino Eggs:** http://www.steampoweredfamily.com/activities/hatch-dinosaur-eggs-with-science/
9. **DIY Conveyor Belt:** http://www.pinkstripeysocks.com/2015/04/how-to-make-conveyor-belt-kids-craft.html
10. **Five Field Kono Game:** http://www.whatdowedoallday.com/2016/05/five-field-kono.html
11. **Dara Game:** http://www.whatdowedoallday.com/2016/05/dara-game.html
12. **Build a Snack Mix Machine:** http://leftbraincraftbrain.com/2016/03/08/stem-challenge-build-snack-mix-machine/

Extension projects for activities found in the **SENSE** chapter:

1. **Digital Flower Still Life:** http://handmadekidsart.com/drawing-flowers/
2. **Play & Learn with Your Food:** http://leftbraincraftbrain.com/category/food/
3. **Spin Art:** http://www.whatdowedoallday.com/2009/02/spin-spin-spin.html
4. **Straw Engineering Project:** http://lemonlimeadventures.com/building-with-straws-engineering-challenge-for-kids/
5. **Gummy Bear Grow Experiment:** http://www.weewarhols.com/gummy-bear-grow-experiment/
6. **Learning Playdough Mats:** http://www.playdoughtoplato.com/100-free-playdough-mats/
7. **Maple Syrup Snow Candy:** http://www.pinkstripeysocks.com/2014/11/maple-syrup-candy-made-using-snow.html
8. **Gelatin Science & Art Project:** http://babbledabbledo.com/science-art-activity-for-kids-gelatin-streaking/
9. **DIY Kazoos:** http://buggyandbuddy.com/exploring-sound-making-a-kazoo-science-invitation-saturday/

///

Extension projects for activities found in the **GROW** chapter:

1. **Homemade Fondant:** http://teachbesideme.com/rock-candy-geodes/
2. **Succulent Terrarium:** http://www.weewarhols.com/valentine-succulent-terrariums/
3. **Plant Lifecycle Activities:** http://www.playdoughtoplato.com/21-plant-life-cycle-activities/
4. **Regrowing Vegetables from Scraps:** http://www.whatdowedoallday.com/2014/04/plant-science-regrowing-vegetables-from-scraps.html gardening-activity-kid-made-plant-markers.html
5. **Sensory Bottles:** http://lemonlimeadventures.com/sensory-bottles-experimenting-with-absorption/
6. **Learning Biology with Homemade Yogurt:** http://leftbraincraftbrain.com/2015/03/31/biology-of-yogurt/
7. **Sun Prints:** http://www.pinkstripeysocks.com/2014/06/diy-sun-prints-with-construction-paper.html
8. **Overnight Crystal Gardens:** http://babbledabbledo.com/science-for-kids-crystal-garden/

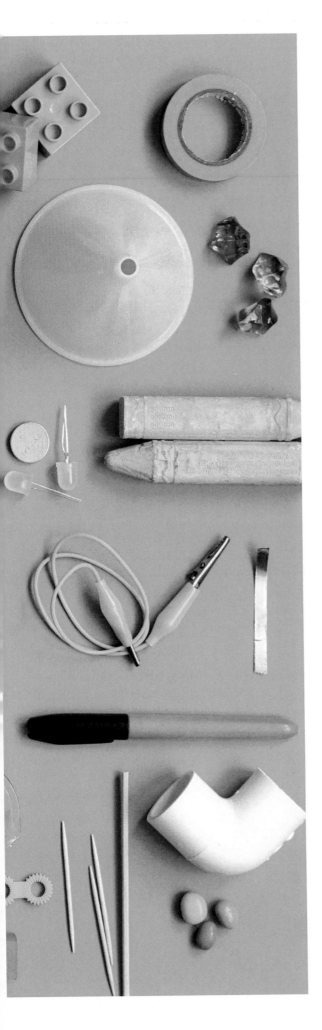

INDEX

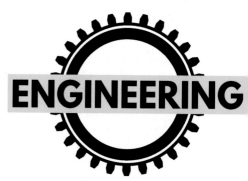

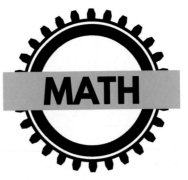

INDEX

Meet the Authors

Anne Carey
Left Brain Craft Brain

Anne is an MIT-educated chemical engineer turned stay-at-home mama who writes about crafty ways to encourage learning in our kids. STEAM projects are her fave.

Follow her on:

Ana Dziengel
Babble Dabble Do

Ana Dziengel is an architect, award winning furniture designer, and blogger. She's now a professional crafter, amateur scientist, and art teacher to her three children.

Follow her on:

Amber Scardino
Wee Warhols

Amber is a mother to two active boys, a blogger and private art teacher / owner of Wee Warhols - Children's Art Classes in Austin, TX.

Follow her on:

Chelsey Marashian
Buggy and Buddy

Chelsey is a former elementary teacher, current stay-at-home mom to two kids. She strives to inspire creativity and self-confidence while promoting learning and fun.

Follow her on:

Dayna Abraham
Lemon Lime Adventures

Dayna is a National Board Certified early childhood teacher turned homeschooling mom of three. She shares ideas for intentional learning from sensory to science.

Follow her on:

Erica Clark
What Do We Do All Day?

Erica is an NYC mom and a children's book and activity blogger. A self-proclaimed theater and book nerd, her two boys have nurtured in her a love of science and math.

Follow her on:

Jamie Hand
Handmade Kids Art

Jamie is a certified art instructor and a mother of three. She writes about quick, easy and inspiring STEAM activities to grow creative kids.

Follow her on:

Karyn Tripp
Teach Beside Me

Karyn is a former educator and current homeschool parent of 4 children. She is passionate about hands-on learning and loves creating unique learning activities for families.

Follow her on:

Leslie Manlapig
Pink Stripey Socks

Leslie has degrees in engineering and psychology. She's a proud mama to two boys and loves crafting, building, and exploring with kiddos!

Follow her on:

Malia Hollowell
Playdough to Plato

Malia is a National Board Certified elementary teacher and Stanford M.Ed. graduate turned website founder who shares addictively fun learning activities for kids.

Follow her on:

P. R. Newton
STEAM Powered Family

Piper has a B.Sc. Psychology degree and has spent many years studying and learning about the human brain. She writes about education and childhood mental health.

Follow her on:

HOW TO USE A STEAM JOURNAL

Use the STEAM Journal to:

Explore Ideas

Sketch Designs

Do Calculations

Use the Scientific Method

Ask a question
Document research
Form a hypothesis
Design an experiment
Record and analyze data
Draw a conclusion

Invent! Create! Dream!

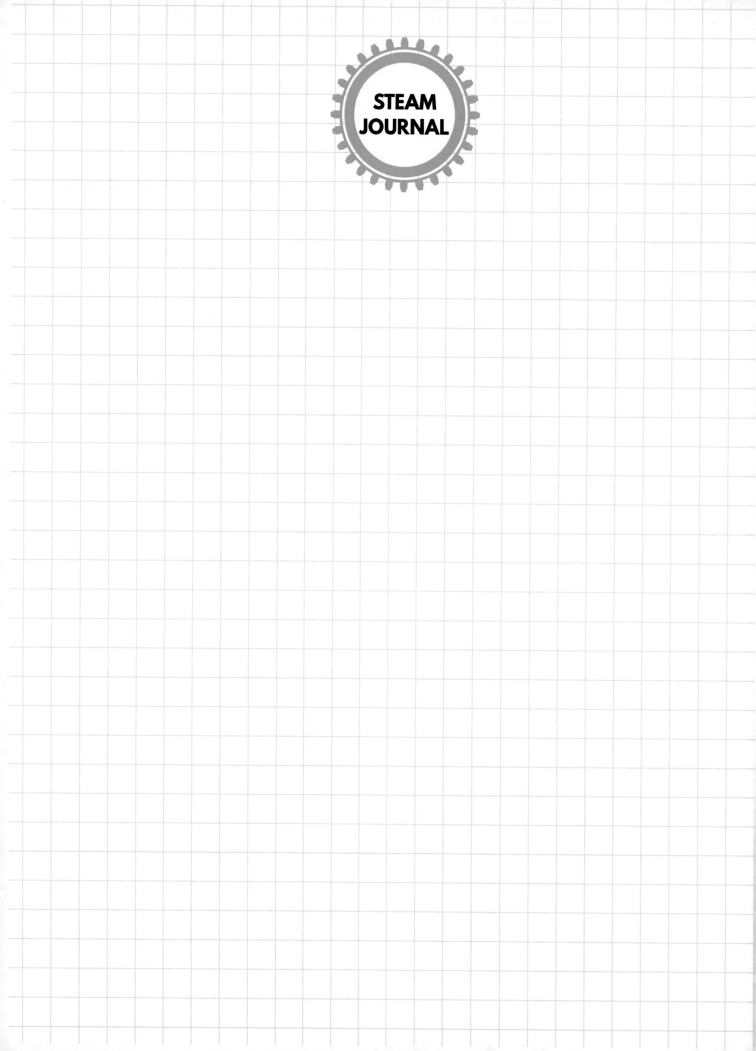

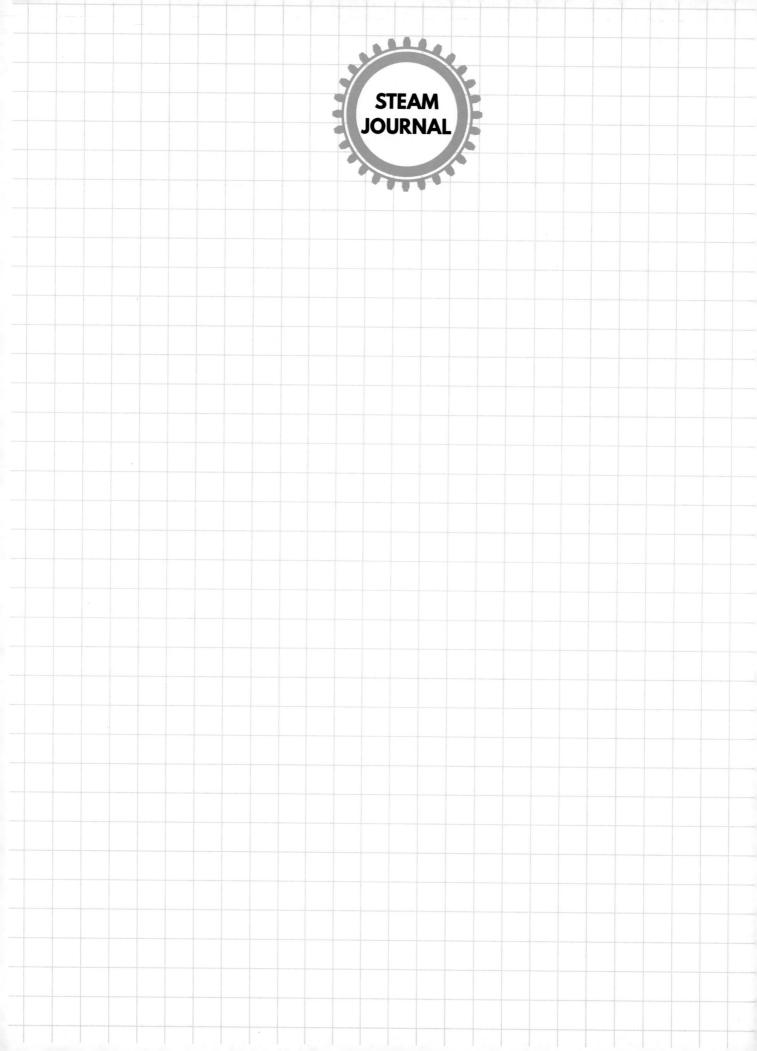

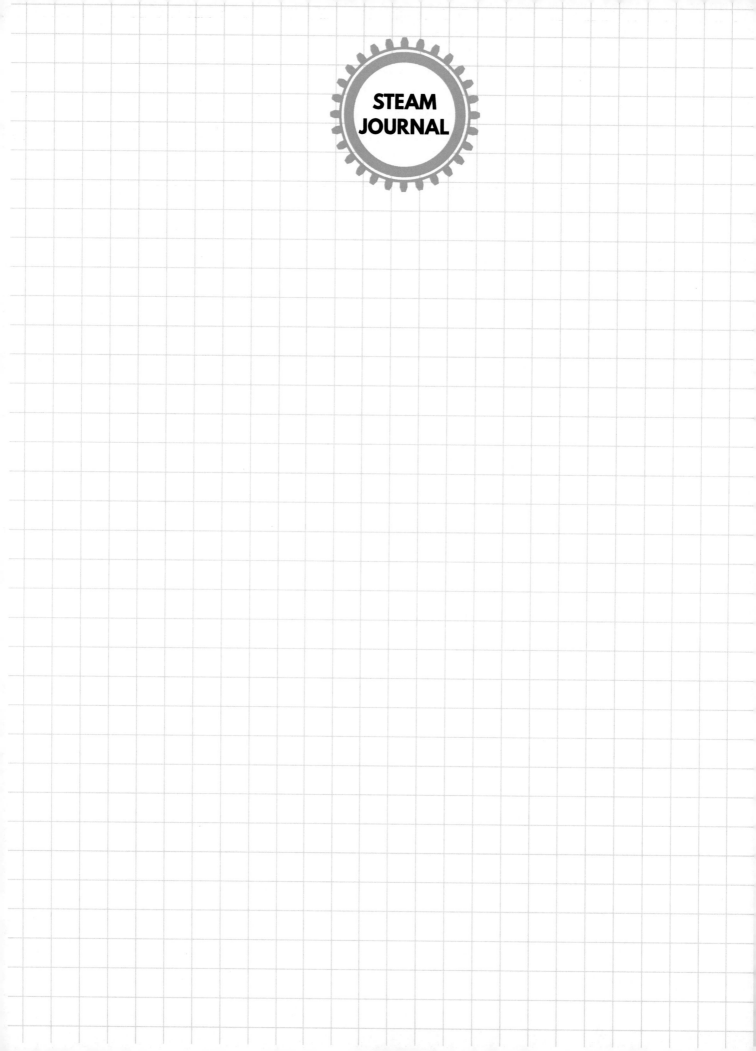

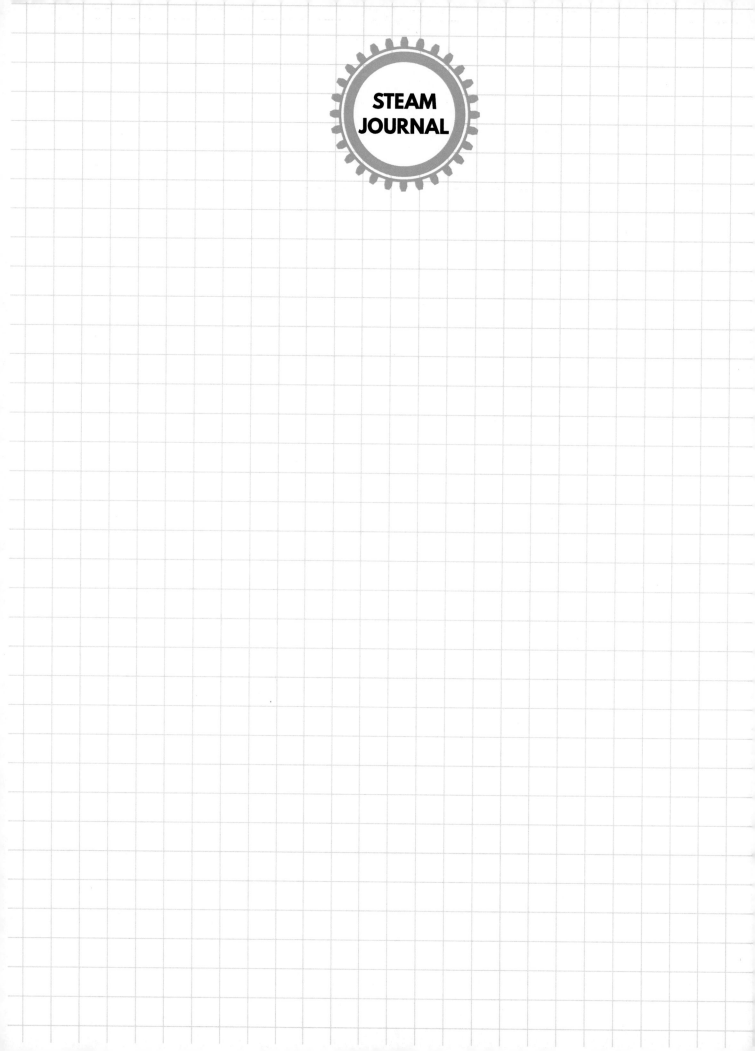

Made in the USA
Middletown, DE
03 March 2017